prayers *for* school teachers

PRAYERS FOR
School Teachers

Contemporary Conversations with God

Sharon M. Harris-Ewing

THE PILGRIM PRESS

CLEVELAND

This book is dedicated to the members of my family
whose love and encouragement have made it happen.
CHUCK, my loving partner in all of life,
our children, **ELAINE** and **BEN**, gifts of God,
whose lives and love are a source of joy beyond words,
and my parents,
JOHN, my mentor in thoughtful faith,
and **LOIS**, the model of a Christian teacher.
And to God,
who has led me through many twists and turns
to become a teacher educator,
and still walks with me
on this lifelong journey in ministry.

The Pilgrim Press, 700 Prospect Avenue, Cleveland, Ohio 44115-1100
thepilgrimpress.com
copyright 2006 by Sharon Harris-Ewing

Printed in the United States of America on acid-free paper

10   09   08   07   06   5   4   3   2   1

Library of Congress Cataloging-in-Publication Data

Harris-Ewing, Sharon M., 1954–
    Prayers for school teachers : contemporary conversations with God   /
Sharon M. Harris-Ewing.
      p. cm.
    ISBN-13: 978-0-8298-1734-8 (alk. paper)
    1. Teachers—Prayer-books and devotions—English.   I. Title.
BV4596.T43H37 2006
242'.88—dc22
                                        2006012895

ISBN-13 : 978-0-8298-1734-8
ISBN-10 : 0-8298-1734-4

CONTENTS

✦ CONTENTS ✦

❈ Preface

I am a teacher educator because of my deep commitment to children. I believe that every student in every school is a child of God and deserves the best education we know how to provide. I am grateful to be a teacher educator at Roberts Wesleyan College because the setting of a Christian liberal arts college allows and even encourages me to make explicit the connection between my commitment to children, children's education, and my Christian faith. I am also thankful for the professional grant I received from the college to support work on this book.

Excellent education requires, first and foremost, outstanding teachers. The ability of a community to provide such education depends upon teachers who have the professional competencies and commitment to promote all students' learning and growth. I strive to teach my students well, caring for and challenging them to learn at the highest levels possible, so that they will be well prepared to become excellent teachers who care for and challenge their students to learn to their fullest potential.

Teacher educators spend significant amounts of time and research effort trying to determine and articulate the specific knowledge, skills, and professional dispositions needed for effective teaching. Such work is ongoing and essential. Christian teacher educators face the added challenge of describing what is distinctive about being a Christian teacher.

My personal response to this question is multifaceted but begins here with an affirmation of the importance of prayer and an offering of prayers to guide and inspire teachers as they pray. Although it is not and never should be a professional requirement or state regulation that teachers approach teaching prayerfully, it is certainly an appropriate goal for Christian teachers that is consistent with personal faith and discipleship. If Christians offer to God in prayer all aspects of their lives, then Christian teachers surely must offer to God in prayer the fullness of their experience as teachers—with all of its joy and challenges.

Over the years my teacher education students have expressed great appreciation for the prayers with which I begin each class. This volume of prayers is one way for me to extend this time of prayer beyond their college classrooms into their lives as classroom teachers. I have written it with a deep and abiding prayer that all who are called to teach will be empowered by the love of God, the grace of Jesus Christ, and the guiding wisdom of the Holy Spirit to be excellent teachers for all of the children whom God sets in their midst.

Sharon Harris-Ewing

INTRODUCTION:
1 ❀ Children in the Midst of Us

Then he took a little child and put it among them;

and taking it in his arms, he said to them,

"Whoever welcomes one such child in my name welcomes me,

and whoever welcomes me welcomes not me but the one who sent me."

—Mark 9:36–37

Children are our future. That sentiment has been expressed in many ways by concerned parents, teachers, social service providers, and even politicians. It is true. The future of our planet depends on many things, including how we care for and educate the people who are now children. The willingness and ability of families and communities to provide adequate nutrition, safe neighborhoods, affordable health care, and high quality education will profoundly affect the people who will be tomorrow's adults. How we nurture their minds, bodies, and spirits will determine their future and our own.

But that is only half of the truth. It is as important to accept responsibility for children because of who they are now—today—as it is to care for them because of who they will become in the future. Children are people God has set among us, people God calls us to welcome and love. Children cannot care for themselves, educate themselves, or even vote on behalf of themselves to ensure that they will receive what they need. It is the responsibility of adults, beginning but not ending with parents, to provide all that children need to grow into the people God intends them to become. The proverbial village required to raise a child includes parents, extended family members, neighborhoods, communities of faith, towns and cities, states and nations.

Christians who take seriously Christ's charge to welcome the children must both accept their role as village members and call upon others to do their part. This means some of us will be providing services directly, in any number of ways, from feeding hungry children to offering day care for working mothers or teaching English language classes for refugee parents. It also means that all of us must be advocates for policies and programs that will create a society that truly values and nurtures the children in our midst.

One of the fundamental ways that every community in the United States fulfills its responsibility to care for children is through its system of formal education, beginning with preschool programs and extending through high school. One of the ways that many individual Christians feel called by God to serve children is through teaching in such programs and schools. These women and men often recount how God has given them the spirit and skills for teaching, and worked through the experiences of their lives to lead them to pursue this noble vocation. Whether in public, religious, or other private schools, their teaching is a form of Christian ministry and an essential component of the community's response to its children.

This book of prayers is for them. It extends an invitation and a challenge to Christian teachers in any setting to approach teaching prayerfully: to pray for themselves, their students, their colleagues, and their community. Within the book are prayers in all of the traditional prayer forms, including songs of thanksgiving, humble confessions, and prayers of petition for oneself and intercession for others. Although some of the prayers are general in nature, others are intentionally and perhaps unusually specific. They are heartfelt conversations with God, intended to inspire the teacher who reads them to be equally immediate and authentic in his or her own prayers. The incarnation of God in Jesus Christ is a gift and a promise that God dwells among us and cares about the very real joys, frustrations, and sorrows of everyday human life. The prayers in this book were written with steadfast faith that God is present in the classroom, God works through teachers to nurture children's growth, and God cares deeply about the successes and struggles that teachers and their students experience each day.

Although the prayers in this book are intended to be meaningful for all who feel called by God to teach in any setting, included among them are strong affirmations of the essential role of public education and explicit prayers for public school leaders. Public schools are the primary means by which every community fulfills its responsibility to children. Public education is a service provided by the whole citizenry free of cost to every child. Like libraries and police protection, the schools are and should be fully supported by everyone—whether or not one ever chooses or needs to use them. Public schools also provide one of the first settings in our society where the rich diversity of people created by God may be experienced. The increasing diversity within the United States is beautifully apparent in the public schools where children rich and poor, children of every race and ethnicity, and children of every language and faith are often seated side by side. These students are given the opportunity to learn together the knowledge and skills needed for living in a global society and the rights and responsibilities of citizenship in this country. They study together the history of our nation and world; they are challenged to make history by living together in a world at peace.

Nevertheless, public schools provide a unique challenge for those seeking to minister in Christ's name through teaching. Funded by public resources and governed by public officials, public schools are government institutions that must comply with the United States Constitution. Consistent with the Establishment Clause of the First Amendment, public schools can do nothing that would establish or endorse one religion over another religion, or even religion over nonreligion. That means, for example, that teachers (and principals and all school leaders) cannot advocate for their religion or lead their students in prayer.

Some Christian teachers react with serious dismay, either because they do not fully comprehend such constitutional prohibitions and why they are as important to Christianity as to all other religious faiths, or because they focus on what they cannot do in the classroom rather than considering the possibilities and power of what they can do. It is beyond the scope of this book to detail all that teachers can and cannot do; in addition to constitutional guidelines and federal regulations, individual school districts have their own policies. However, the foundational assumption of this book of prayers is that the three most important things Christian teachers can do to minister in Christ's name are things they are allowed to do in all schools, whether public, religious, or private.

Christians are called to model the love of God in Christ, to use their God-given talents in service to others, and to pray without ceasing. In any school Christian teachers can—and should—model the love of God in every interaction with others: with students, parents, colleagues, supervisors, and public officials; in classrooms, hallways, cafeterias, offices, and boardrooms. In the words of the great contemporary hymn, "they'll know we are Christians by our love." In any school Christian teachers can—and should—develop and utilize the abilities and experiences God has given them to become effective teachers who help every student learn at the highest levels possible.

In any school Christian teachers can—and should—offer sincere prayers for their students, the school community, and themselves as they teach each day. This book may be thought of as an answer to the question, "But how shall I pray?" It is a collection of prayers for teachers in any school setting as they teach through the seasons of the school year and their own lives. If it serves its purpose as God intends, the book will be only a first response because those reading it will not stop here, but will continue to answer the question for the rest of their lives. Those who are called to teach are called to pray without ceasing.

2 ❁ Prayers of Thanksgiving

Welcoming the Children

God incarnate in Jesus Christ,
you came to earth as a child.
You welcomed children with open arms.
You claim us as your children.

Thank you, God.
Thank you for the gift of children.
Thank you for the boundless energy of growing bodies,
for curious minds longing to learn.
Thank you for hearts awed by the wonders of your world,
for spirits open wide to receive your love.

Thank you for the gift of children.
Thank you for the child in me.

Teach me to welcome children in your name.
Teach me to live as a child of God. In your name.
Amen.

Yes! Every Age Is a Great Age

For grinning faces and wide-open eyes.
For skipping down the hall and laughing out loud.
For spaghetti in hair and popsicles melting on hands.
For mud-stained pants and sneakers that blink.
For feet that stomp and arms that hug.
For every ooh and aah at the wonder of your world.
For every hand raised high to give the answer.
For every "why?" that seeks understanding.
Thank you, God, for the gift of children.

For faces with acne and eyes with mascara.
For running the bases and dancing to music.
For bright-colored hair and car keys in hand.
For blue jeans too big and T-shirts too small.
For feet in high heels and arms raised in protest.
For every no to injustice and yes to life.
For every hand extended to offer help to another.
For every "why?" that seeks understanding.
Thank you, God, for the gift of teenagers.

For faces of hope and eyes growing wise.
For going to college and getting a job.
For hair that is styled and hands on the keyboard.
For sweatpants in class and suits at the office.
For feet that travel far and arms that hold loved ones near.
For every struggle to choose a career and partner for life.
For every hand that pushes a lever to vote.
For every "why?" that seeks understanding.
Thank you, God, for the gift of young adults.
Amen.

The Darndest Things

God of all ages and stages,
I'm revealing my age
to say that I remember
Art Linkletter's
Kids Say the Darndest Things.
It's trite, but true.
They do!

Thank you, God,
for the
crazy
wonderful
fun
incredible
touching
revealing
silly
amazing
things
that kids say.

Their words,
their perspectives,
their hugs
are such a gift in my life.
All gifts come from you.
Thank you, God.
Amen.

The Gift of Music

Make a joyful noise unto the Lord.

Learning to make music
using one's voice,
pressing lips and blowing through a horn,
moving the bow gently across violin strings,
tapping black and white piano keys.
The band on stage,
the band marching across football fields.
The orchestra and the chorus.

Learning to appreciate music,
to read notes on a staff,
to hear the harmony of voices joined in song,
to unravel the mysteries of music theory,
to be moved by the beauty of sound and power of lyrics,
to explore the diversity of music
spanning human history and contemporary culture.

Opportunities for students of all ages
to discover and develop new talents,
to learn the wonders of a vast new world,
to make a joyful noise, to hear a joyful noise.

We give you thanks and praise, O Lord,
for the gift of music in all of its glorious forms.

Help us to ensure that
every student in every school
has opportunities to learn
to make music and to appreciate music.
May their school experiences
be but the beginning
of a lifetime of loving music
and loving you through music. Amen.

All Roads Led to Teaching

Thank you, God, for the call to teach.

Thank you for the gifts I need for teaching:
a mind eager to learn,
the ability to communicate in speech and writing,
a heart full of love for students,
the persistence to explain and demonstrate and re-teach
again and again until they understand,
a spirit of humility.

Thank you for all the experiences in my life
that have prepared me to become a teacher:
lessons of life, learned in school and out,
role models whose enthusiastic teaching inspired me,
opportunities to explore how best to use my gifts,
mentors who encouraged and guided me,
faith in you and salvation in Christ.

You are amazing.
You are the giver of my gifts.
You are the guide of my experiences.
You are the weaver.
You have woven together the gifts and experiences of my life
into a beautiful, multicolored tapestry of teaching.
I feel your hand. I see your handiwork.
Thank you, God, for the call to teach.
Amen.

For the Love of Learning

Learning.
Increased knowledge.
New skills.
Creative thinking.
Alternative ways to solve problems.
Deeper understanding of others.
Greater appreciation for the wonders of the universe.

The more I learn,
the more I see how much there is to learn,
the more I want to learn.
The more I learn,
the more I am awed
by the miracle of life itself
from the tiniest particle of matter
to the unfathomable vastness of space.
The more I learn,
the more I am amazed
by the divine gift
of the human drive to learn.
The more I learn,
the more I know and love you, God.

Spectacular God,
You are the Creator of all there is to learn.
You are the Spirit alive in my quest to learn.
You are the Source of my love for learning.

Magnificent God,
Accept my praise and thanksgiving for the gift of learning.
Hear my prayer of hope for a lifetime of loving to learn.
Use my learning and my teaching to inspire others
to love learning, too.
Amen.

For Learning To Teach

God, I confess.
I didn't think there was so much to it.
I love children.
I thought teaching would be easy.
But going to school to learn to teach
taught me otherwise.
Teaching is time-consuming, hard work,
and I had to work hard to learn how to do it.

God, I thank you.
For all that I have learned.
For professors who practiced what they preached
and modeled good teaching.
For instructors who did not make it easy
but challenged me to study diligently and think deeply.
For every opportunity
to observe a classroom,
to practice a new skill,
to master complex concepts,
to receive valuable feedback
about how to improve what I was doing.

God, I ask you.
Please keep my mind and heart open
to keep learning
how to teach,
how to be the always improving,
reflective
effective teacher
you have called me to become
for the sake of the children I love
as you love me.
Amen.

For the Love of Teaching

Teaching.
It's a challenge.
Hard work. Time consuming.
Tiring. Sometimes so frustrating.
Teaching is a challenge,
but I love it.
Engaging. Stimulating.
Rewarding. Sometimes so wonder-full.
To know that
I can make a difference in someone else's life
makes all the difference in my life.

I know there is a lot of work
that I would not like to do.
I know there are a lot of people
who do not like the work they do.

I feel so lucky.
I love my work.
I feel so blessed.
I am a teacher, and
I love teaching.

Thank you, God,
for the amazing gift of work that I love.
Thank you, God,
for the divine blessing of being a teacher.
Amen.

The Art and Science of Teaching

My professor said that teaching is an art and a science.
She was right.

God of the Artist,
whose Spirit inspires works of human art,
God of creativity and imagination, love and hope,
thank you for the art of teaching.

Thank you that my teaching is unique.
At its best,
it is an expression of the person I am, inspired by you,
a creative response to the teachable moment,
a loving reflection of the person you have led me to become.
It is heeding my call to teach each day
with flexibility, imagination, and hope.
God of the Artist,
keep the art in my teaching,
make my teaching the best it can be.

God of the Scientist,
whose Spirit inspires human minds to seek understanding,
God of all knowledge and wisdom, reason and judgment,
thank you for the science of teaching.

Thank you that my teaching can be based upon sound evidence,
meaningful research about how students develop and learn.
At its best,
it is the thoughtful implementation of practices that work,
a commitment to know and use
what is known about teaching and learning,
a willingness to continually assess and revise what I'm doing.
It is heeding my call to teach each day
with understanding, wisdom, and judgment.
God of the Scientist,

keep the science in my teaching,
make my teaching the best it can be.

In the name of Christ who calls me to be the best I can be.
Amen.

For Great Role Models

God revealed in human history,
you sent Jesus the Christ
to save us through your incredible love for us,
to teach us how to live according to your will.
Jesus is my savior and my teacher,
the ultimate role model for
loving and teaching and living with faith.

God revealed in my life,
I believe that you have also sent
human role models
to love me deeply and teach me well,
to awaken my love of learning,
to inspire me to love and teach others,
to show me how to teach and live with faith.

Thank you, God, for
these great teachers in my life,
dedicated women and men
whose life lessons remain in my mind,
whose spirits enliven my heart,
whose models I seek to follow,
whose names I lift up to you in prayer.

Thank you, God, for
all that I have learned from them,
all that I continue to learn from them.

Use me, God,
that I might be such a role model for others,
loving and teaching my students,
inspiring them to learn and to love,
showing them how to love and live with faith.

Thank you, God, for Jesus Christ, who is
my savior, my teacher, my greatest role model.
In his name. Amen.

For Teacher Educators

Designer of the human mind,
with all of its power and imagination,
Sculptor of the human heart,
with all of its potential for love and hate,
thank you for the capacity
to seek understanding
of how our minds work and learn,
of how our hearts can be shaped for good.

Thank you for scientists
who study how our brains function.
Thank you for researchers
who investigate how we learn.
Thank you for educators
who examine the development
of character and moral virtue.

Thank you for teacher educators
who use what they have learned from others,
as well as the results of their own research
and the wisdom of their own experience,
to teach others how to teach
so that all children will have

every opportunity to learn and grow
in mind and heart as you intend.

Thank you for what I have learned
from teacher educators
before I began teaching and since.
Guide them as they continue
to study and learn, and teach others.
Guide me as I continue
to study and learn, and teach others.
Guide us all to teach as you desire,
with open minds and loving hearts. Amen.

Always and Everywhere

Thank you, God,
for the gift of your presence
always and everywhere.

Thank you for the assurance
that you are with me in all that I do:
as I write my lesson plans,
as I welcome students each day,
as I stand in front of them to explain, and
as I sit with them to solve problems.

Thank you for the promise
that you are with me whatever I am feeling:
when I am eager and excited,
when I am discouraged and depressed,
when I am confident about my teaching, and
when I am not at all sure what I am doing.

Thank you for the certainty
that you are with me when I work with others:

students who are struggling and
students who are soaring;
parents who are neglectful and
parents who are nurturing;
colleagues who complain and
colleagues who collaborate;
administrators who criticize and
administrators who cheer me on.

Thank you for the comfort
that comes from knowing
you are with me when I am alone.

God, you are present
always and everywhere.
Help me to feel your presence,
to be led by your Spirit,
to share your love
always and everywhere.
Amen.

For the Gift of Faith in Times of Trouble

Thank you, God,
for the faith that sustains me
when all else fails.

When there's chaos at home,
and my students are acting crazy,
and the principal is on my case,
and my salary doesn't cover the bills,
when nothing seems to be going right,
thank you, God,
for the faith that gets me through.

When I forget my lesson plans,
and I can't seem to get students' papers graded,
and I lose my patience with parents,
and I don't know how to answer students' questions,
when I really am not sure that I should be a teacher,
thank you, God,
for the faith that keeps me going.

I have faith that
I have been saved by your grace alone,
through Jesus your Son, my Savior.
I have faith that
I can walk each day in the presence of your Holy Spirit,
guided and upheld
through times of joy and times of trouble.

Thank you, God,
for the only thing that sustains me when all else fails,
amazing grace,
the gift of my faith.
In Jesus' name.
Amen.

Those Who Pray for Me

Mighty and Merciful God,
who blesses us with the gift of prayer,
who listens with love when we pray:

Today my prayer
is a prayer of thanksgiving
for the people who pray for me, and
for the prayers they have offered.

Thank you for family and friends
and colleagues at school
who include me in their prayers each day.

Thank you for the people of my church
when they gather for worship
and remember to pray
for all the children of our community, and
for the parents and teachers and counselors
who nurture children's growth and learning.

Thank you for everyone, known and unknown,
who lifts to you their prayers for me
when I have a special need
for guidance or healing or comfort or hope.

Thank you that I am surrounded by
people who love me enough to pray for me,
people who love you enough to pray for me.
I feel the power of their prayer.
I feel the power of your love working in my life,
giving me energy and direction, healing and hope.
I believe that these people are your servants,
their prayers are channels of your love and grace.

Mighty and Merciful God,
My life—and my teaching—are blessed by others
and the prayers they offer on my behalf.
May I be as faithful in my prayers for them
as they have been in their prayers for me.
Amen.

3 ❀ Prayers for Forgiveness

The Lone Ranger

Merciful God,
when I pause to consider
how you have worked in the world,
how you have worked in my life,
I am speechless with shame.

You do not work alone.
You have spoken in human history
through prophets and apostles.
You have shared your redeeming love for humankind
through your Son, Jesus the Christ.
You have touched my life
through the loving words and prayerful guidance
of more people than I could ever name.

Forgive me for trying to go it alone.
Forgive me for thinking that I can teach all by myself.

Remind me, O God, how much I need others to help me teach:
students who open their minds and hearts to receive me,
parents and guardians who partner with me to help each student,
colleagues who share their experiences, ideas, and strategies,

leaders who empower me, family and friends who support me.

Remind me, O God, how much I need you to help me teach:
loving, guiding, sustaining, equipping, healing, saving me.

God, who is my ever-present help,
forgive me for trying to go it alone.
Amen.

∽

When I Fail to See

God who seeks and saves the lost,
God who rejoices when one lost sheep is found,
forgive me
when I fail to see the lost children in my class,
when I fail to teach them well
because I do not seek and see them.

Forgive me
when I fail to notice the quiet child,
when I fail to accept the disfigured child,
when I fail to expect much from the child who is poor,
when I fail to respond to the child who is troubled,
when I fail to reach out to the child without friends,
when I fail to challenge the gifted child,
when I fail to include the child with disabilities.

Forgive me
when I fail to accept as a gift from you
every child in my class,
when I fail to teach to the very limits of my ability
every student entrusted to me.

God who seeks and saves the lost,
you have sought me, and found me.
Hear my prayer for

a heart that is willing
and eyes that are able
to seek and see and teach
the lost children in my class.
Amen.

I Lost My Temper

Merciful God,
I confess.
I lost it today.
I won't make excuses.
I won't try to justify it.
I won't pretend that what was wrong is right.
I got angry.
I yelled.
I said things I regret.
I hurt others.
God of steadfast love and mercy, forgive me.

I repent.
Show me another way.
Help me to understand what happened,
to make amends . . . to learn from it.

God of steadfast love and mercy, forgive me.
Show me another way . . . your way.
Amen.

I Didn't Do My Homework

Just like my students
who have endless explanations for
why they did not do their homework,

I can recite all kinds of reasons
why I did not plan my lesson,
why I came to school today
not prepared to teach.

None of my excuses is adequate.
Yes. I am busy.
There's a lot on my plate.
But I know that
good teaching requires planning.
And I know that
my students deserve good teaching.

God, you know
what I need to do,
what I make time to do,
and what I leave undone.

God, forgive me
when I am not ready,
when I am unprepared
to be the effective teacher
you have called me to become.

God, guide me
to use my time carefully,
so that I will make time
to plan my lessons well,
and be a good teacher
who respects students
and uses their time carefully.

God, empower me
to get my homework done.
Amen.

Acknowledging My Arrogance

God revealed in Jesus Christ,
Christ who came not to be served, but to serve,
Spirit of the last who shall be first,
forgive me
when I start to think too highly of myself.

Forgive me
when I think I know so much about teaching
that I don't have any more to learn.
Forgive me
when I think I am such a superior teacher
that I don't have to listen to others' suggestions.
Forgive me
when I think I am so important
that I don't have to value the people around me.
Forgive me
when I start to think too highly of myself.

Spirit of service and humility,
Open my eyes to see how much I have to learn.
Open my ears to hear all that others can teach me.
Open my heart to value others as you value them.
Amen.

When It's My Turn to Forgive

God by whose grace I have been forgiven,
Christ who commands that I forgive seventy-times-seven times,
Spirit of forgiveness beyond counting,
show me when it's my turn.
Teach me to forgive others.

Give me grace to forgive students
whose words hurt me,
whose homework is not done because of chaos at home,
whose defiance is a mask for their fear of failure,
whose lack of attention is beyond their control,
whose clothes smell because they are the only ones they own.

Give me grace to forgive parents
who are overeager and come to school too much,
who don't know how to help and come to school too little,
who discourage their children by expecting too much,
who hold their children back by expecting too little,
who cannot give their children the gift of hope
because they themselves have none.

Give me grace to forgive colleagues
when they are competing instead of collaborating,
when they forget to communicate what others need to know,
when they set a bad example for students, knowingly or not,
when stress in their own lives keeps them from teaching well,
when conflicts among us distract us
from doing what we're here to do.

Ever-faithful, forgiving God,
I know what you want me to do.
You have shown me.
Teach me to forgive others. In your name.
Amen.

Forgiving Myself

Sometimes the hardest person to forgive is myself.
I do things I know I shouldn't.
I say things I wish I hadn't.
I fail to do things I know I should.
I waste time on things that don't matter,
so there's no time left for things that do.
I hurt others. I hurt myself.
At school. And at home.

God who knows all,
you know my heart.
You know what I am trying to do even when I don't succeed.
You know who I am trying to be even when I falter.
You know that I am striving to do my best each day.
At school. And at home.

By the power of your Word,
help me to trust in the promise of your forgiveness.
By the power of your Spirit,
help me to feel forgiven.
By the power of your love,
teach me to forgive myself
because you have already forgiven me
through Jesus who is the Christ.
Amen.

My Harshest Critic

Oh God. I am hurting.
I am my own harshest critic.
Perhaps that sounds like hyperbole,
even so it feels like truth,
painful truth.

Creator God, you made me.
Wanting to use the gifts you have given
to be the best teacher I can be
is a worthy goal.

Redeemer God, you saved me.
Thinking I have to be perfect,
holding myself to an impossible standard,
is a sinful goal
because it denies your grace
and separates me from your salvation.
Is it ironic? or just obvious?
"Beating myself up"
about the failures and inadequacies
that I see too clearly, too obsessively
does not help, but rather prevents me
from becoming the best teacher I can be.

Spirit God, you are present now and always
to forgive the flaws, to heal the pain,
to guide me as I learn to live a new way.

Holy God,
I repent. Forgive me.
I want to change. Show me how.
Yes. I will continue to strive
to do my best, to be the best teacher I can be.
Yes. I will also strive to be the best learner I can be,
learning from you how to forgive myself.
Forgiven, healed, guided by your grace
I will grow. Thank you, God.
Amen.

This prayer was written after a particularly "unsuccessful" day of teaching.

4 ❋ Prayers for Guidance

That I Might Be Your Instrument

God whose power created the earth and all its inhabitants,
God whose wisdom has guided people throughout history,
God whose love saves people in all places and times:

I am a teacher.
Make me an instrument of your creative power:
that I might awaken in my students a lifelong passion for learning,
that I might form of my students a caring community of learners,
that I might discover how to reach students
who are struggling in whatever way.

I am a teacher.
Make me an instrument of your guiding wisdom:
that I might nurture the development of students young and old,
that I might teach the truths that matter for a lifetime,
that I might model the life that I have learned
from the Bible and saints of faith.

I am a teacher.
Make me an instrument of your saving love:
that I might receive and accept all my students just as they are,
that I might care for them as whole people,
growing in mind and heart and body,

that I might teach them to love themselves and their neighbors . . .
by the example I set

God, I am a teacher.
Use me . . . use even me
to be an instrument of your power, wisdom, and love,
now and forever.
Amen.

∞

Planting Seeds

A teacher plants seeds.
Wonder.
A world to explore.
Curiosity.
Questions to answer.
Compassion.
Problems to solve.
Patience.
Perseverance.
Hope.

A teacher tends the soil.
Nourishment.
Warmth.
Openness to air.
Light.
Refreshment of rain.
Encouragement.
Patience.
Perseverance.
Hope.

God gives the growth.

God of all life,
guide me as I plant the seeds
and tend the soil of my classroom.
Give me patience and trust
as I watch and wait
for my students to learn and grow,
each one in his or her own time.
Grant me a humble heart and hands
as you guide their growth.
Amen.

High Expectations

All-Knowing God,
you know me better than I know myself.
You know my students better than I can ever know them.
Help me, God, to know how much to expect of them.

I know that I will communicate my expectations to students,
sometimes in ways that I know and want,
sometimes in ways that I don't know or realize.

I know that it is important to have high expectations
for my students.
If I have high expectations, they will achieve more.
If I have low expectations, they will achieve less.

But still I am uncertain.
I fear that if my expectations are too high,
they will not succeed, and
they will think they are "dumb."
I fear that if my expectations are too low,
they will succeed too easily, and
they will think that I think they are "dumb."

What are high expectations? What are low expectations?
What is too much? What is too little? What is fair?
Help me, God, to find answers to my questions.
Help me, God, to set expectations for my students
that are high and fair.
Help me, God, to set expectations for myself that are high and fair.

I pray in the name of Jesus Christ,
who shows me how to live your will,
who expects me to do nothing less.
Amen.

∽

Nurturing the Whole Child

Magnificent Creator,
you sculpted earth and sky.
You breathed life into man and woman.
You declared the goodness of creation.
God in Christ Jesus,
you came to earth in a newborn babe.
By your incarnation in human form
you proclaimed the unity of creation.
Spirit, mind, and body are good.
Spirit, mind, and body are one.

I am challenged to teach students
the skills required of our culture,
the reservoir of human knowledge.
I am privileged to shape their minds
to help them develop thinking skills,
both critical and creative.

Help me to resist the temptation
to so focus on students' minds
that I neglect the rest of their being.

Show me how to teach the whole child,
to engage the heart as well as the mind,
to promote physical and emotional health,
to teach appreciation for art and music,
to encourage stewardship of the earth's resources,
to inspire commitment to justice and peace,
to open doors to the world of faith,
to nurture respect and positive relationships
with other people, alike and different.

God who created us good,
God whose love makes us whole,
help me to see the goodness of every student.
Help me to nurture the wholeness of each one.
Amen.

Patience Is a Divine Virtue

Everlasting, Everloving God,
with patience you entered into relationship with your people.
With patience you taught them how to live.
With patience you still wait for them to return to you.

Everlasting, Everloving God,
teach me patience.
Teach me to slow the pace of instruction
to fit the pace of students' learning.
Teach me to stop and listen
when they are trying to tell me something.
Teach me to let go of my plans
when meeting their immediate needs is more important.

Teach me patience.
Teach me to wait long enough

to let my students think when I ask them a question.
Teach me to repeat myself cheerfully
when they are struggling to learn something new.
Teach me to teach in a different way
when the first way is not working.

Teach me patience.
Teach me to reserve judgment
until I've heard all sides of the story.
Teach me to hold my tongue
when speaking will only make matters worse.
Teach me to trust in you even
when it seems that my prayers have gone unanswered.

God who is patient with me,
teach me to be patient with my students.
Amen.

To Reach the Lost and Lonely

God who seeks to save every child,
God who rejoices to find the one who is lost,
hear my prayer for the lonely, lost child in my class.

She sits alone.
He does not have a friend.
She stares out the window.
He sleeps at his desk.
She plays by herself.
He daydreams.
She will not look at me.
He rejects others because
they first rejected him.

God, save this child.
Give her friends.
Give him the ability to focus.
Give her hope.
Give him the ability to trust others.

God, use me as an instrument of your saving power.
Give me insight
to show your understanding.
Give me compassion
to show your love and create a loving community.
Show me the way
to reach each lonely, lost child in my class.
Amen.

Equity and Excellence

God, this is hard.

I believe in equity *and* excellence.
I want to be fair to all my students.
I want to challenge them all
to achieve at the highest levels possible.
I know what all that does not mean.
I know that treating them fairly
does not mean treating them equally.
I know that the call to excellence
is not a call to sameness.
But what does all that mean?

God, please help me to figure it out.
Help me to understand.
Help me to acknowledge
the differences among my students:

different abilities, different needs,
different disabilities, different personalities.

God who sent Jesus
to teach us what you expect of us,
show me how to be fair to each
and to challenge all.
Show me how to teach them
to live up to the high expectations
that you have for all of us.
In Jesus' name. Amen.

The Teachable Moment

The teachable moment. The kairos.

A student asks a question
to which the teacher does not know the answer.
An opportunity to teach about research tools.

A home in the neighborhood is destroyed by fire.
An opportunity to reach out in service to others.

A disagreement between two students begins to escalate.
An opportunity to practice conflict resolution.

A student in a wheelchair joins the class.
An opportunity to learn about accessibility.

A classroom pet dies.
An opportunity to talk about the life cycle.

A flood destroys vast acres of farmland.
An opportunity to study the forces of nature.

A teacher makes a mistake and catches it.
An opportunity to model learning from failure.

The teachable moment.
When circumstances come together
to provide a unique opportunity for learning.
Perhaps not what was planned,
but still what is important.

God who entered ordinary time
with the extraordinary gift of Jesus Christ,
in the ordinary days of teaching in my class,
help me to be open to see extraordinary moments.

Give me eyes to recognize the teachable moment.
Give me wisdom to seize the moment as an opportunity
to teach and learn something important. Amen.

A Fresh Start

God who forgives us again and again,
God who lets us start over again and again,
teach me to forgive my students.
Teach me to let them begin again. And again.
Amen.

To Give Effective Feedback

Perfect God of amazing grace,
who deals so lovingly with imperfect humanity,
who does not deal with us according to our sin,
but continually invites us to become better than we are
and shows us the way through Jesus the Christ:

Teach me to deal lovingly with my students,
to invite them to increase their learning and improve their work,
and to show them the way through the feedback I give.

Feedback that is
honest,
immediate,
specific,
constructive.
Feedback that
begins with what is positive,
identifies what needs improvement,
provides direction,
promotes learning and growth.

I know that
such feedback is
effective and essential,
but it is not always easy
to find the words
that a student will be able to hear,
or to say the words
that a student may not want to hear.

God of grace,
fill me with your loving Spirit.
Teach me
how to give effective feedback
to my students. Amen.

Religion in the Curriculum

God of wisdom, Spirit of love,
you know my mind and heart,
you know . . . I was surprised.
The social studies curriculum this year includes religion.
I have to teach my students
about Hinduism, Judaism, Buddhism, Christianity, and Islam.

This is an important opportunity
to increase their understanding and respect
for people and faiths that are different from their own.
This is a challenge and a huge responsibility.
I don't know if I'm ready.

I have to learn more
before I will be prepared to teach.
I have to plan ahead
to know how to say things
that will demonstrate understanding and respect,
that will convey accurately and sensitively
the perspectives of people whose beliefs are different from my own.
I have to be careful to talk about Christian faith
in the same way that I discuss other faiths,
with appreciation, without arrogance or bias.

God of wisdom, Spirit of love,
this is an opportunity, and a challenge,
and an important responsibility.
Guide my learning
so that my mind will be ready.
Shape my spirit,
so that my heart will be ready.
This year I have to teach my students
about the many ways that people worship you.
Amen.

To Think Outside the Box

God the Creator,
Author of creativity,
who surprises us
with the outside-the-box,

unexpected, undeserved
gift of love and salvation
in a newborn
laying in a manger,
of all places!
Who could have imagined it?
Only you.

God the Creator,
fill me with your Spirit of creativity.
Whether I am planning lessons,
working with students or parents,
teaching new topics,
solving classroom conflicts, or
searching for something to re-ignite
my own enthusiasm for teaching,
inspire me
to think outside the box!

God the Creator,
who creates and re-creates me,
give me eyes willing to see all the possibilities.
Give me ears willing to listen to others' novel ideas.
Give me hands willing to explore using new materials.
Give me feet willing to go places I have never been.
Give me a mind willing to hear every side of an issue.
Give me the will to consider doing something differently
even when others insist,
"but we've never done it that way before."

God the Creator,
inspire me to think outside the box.
Amen.

Loving the Person, Hating the Behavior

Thank you, God.
The psalmist assures us.
You do not deal with us according to our sin.
Jesus promised us.
In his name, we are forgiven.
Paul reminds us.
While we were yet sinners, Christ died for us.

Help me, God.
Show me how to distinguish
the sin from the sinner,
the behavior from the person.
Show me how to accept and forgive
students with serious behavior problems.
He is hostile and hurtful.
She is angry and argumentative.
He acts out. She skips school.
Their attitudes and actions
prevent them from learning, and
interfere with others' learning, too.
Show me how to love the person
no matter how much I hate the behavior.

Help me, God.
Show me how to love my students
as you have loved me
because you have loved me.
In the name of Jesus the Christ,
who shows me your love.
Amen.

What Resilience Means to Me

God who cares for every child,
God who uses caring adults to show divine love,
God who uses teachers as instruments of grace,
use me.

There are children
who seem to have everything going against them,
young people
who do not seem to have a chance in the world.
Psychologists call them risk factors . . . they are
born to parents who are uneducated, unemployed, in prison,
living in poverty, moving a lot,
absent, uninvolved in school, earning poor grades.

The amazing thing is that some of them beat the odds.
They believe in themselves.
They find a way to succeed in school.
They set goals and work toward them.
They find a way to succeed in life.
Psychologists call them resilient.

What makes the difference?
So often it is a caring adult
who has given time and energy and heart
to build a strong relationship with an individual student,
to support and encourage her, but also
to hold him accountable for meeting high expectations.

God who cares for me,
let me be that caring adult for the student at risk in my class.
God who uses teachers,
let me be an instrument of your grace.
Amen.

Hanging in There

Persistent God,
who never gives up on anyone,
do not let me give up on my students . . . ever.
Amen.

∞

Dealing with Differences

Hanging on a wall in my home
is an old and tattered poster
with an anonymous saying,
"If we accept the premise
that all people are special,
we are better able to deal
with individual differences
in different individuals."

God, I believe.
All people are special.
They are special because
you created them, each and every one.
God, help me to live what I believe.

As a teacher
I work with many individuals:
students, parents, and colleagues.
I encounter what seems to me
to be an infinite number
of individual differences
among these different individuals:
abilities and disabilities,
personalities and temperaments,
interests and traditions,

races and religions,
cultures and languages,
hopes and dreams,
shapes and sizes and skin colors,
and just plain quirky ways!

God, I believe.
All people are special.
Help me to live what I believe,
to deal lovingly
with individual differences
in different individuals
because you created them,
because you created me,
because you love us all. Amen.

To Use Time Wisely

Some people think teaching is easy.
It's nine to three, nine months a year.
But, of course, it isn't.

Teaching takes time during the day,
time with students,
time to set up activities in the classroom,
time to plan with colleagues.
Teaching takes time at night,
time to grade papers,
time to return phone calls,
time to get ready for the next day.
Teaching takes time during the week,
time to do report cards,
time to meet with parents,
time to go to meetings and seminars

and continuing education opportunities,
both required and chosen.
Teaching takes time during the summer,
time to prepare for the year ahead.

God of all time,
help me to use time wisely
so that I will have time
to get done what needs to be done
and do it well.
Help me to use time wisely
so that I will also have time
to care for my own family,
to nurture treasured friendships.
Help me to use time wisely
so that I will have time for myself,
time to exercise and rest my body,
time to relax and refresh my mind,
time to worship
in daily moments of praise and petition,
and weekly gatherings with other believers.

God who gives the gift of time,
teach me to use time wisely. Amen.

Some Classes

O God, my God,
you know my need before I speak it,
you hear my prayer before I offer it.
HELP!

I am at my wit's end.
I don't know all the reasons

but this class is harder than most.
I've heard it said that
every class is unique,
a group of diverse students
with its own personality.
I've found that to be true.
And this one takes the cake.

I'm not sure why it's so hard.
Maybe it's me,
concerns in my own life
that are limiting my effectiveness.
Maybe it's them,
a crazy mix of characters
who simply don't work well together.
Maybe it's something else
I can't identify.
Whatever the reasons,
I need your help.

O God, my God,
give me the patience I need
to deal gently with my own frustration
and lovingly with my students.
Give me the hope I need
to look forward with confidence
and lovingly toward my students.
Give me the wisdom I need
to teach effectively and lovingly—
yes, even this most difficult class.
O God, you know my need.
I know you hear my prayer.
Thank you, God, for your help. Amen.

Keeping Confidence

Sometimes I receive
information about others
in confidence.

A student or a parent
or a colleague
trusts me enough
to share intimate details
of personal pain.
OR
A parent or school colleague
or community professional
must share something
that is sensitive and private
because it will help me
to understand a student,
to teach more responsively,
and thus, more effectively.
OR
Someone repeats what
he has seen, or she has heard
even when
it should not be repeated.

However such information
comes to me,
to know others' secrets
is a privilege and a responsibility,
a sacred trust.

God, save me from the temptation
of sharing with others
even inadvertently

information shared with me
in confidence.
God, guide my words and deeds
that I might be found worthy
of the trust given to me.
God, you are faithful to me.
Make me faithful to others. Amen.

When I Need Help

Faithful God,
you have promised to hear my prayer.
You have promised me the help I need
to do what you have called me to do.

Forgive me, God,
when I fail to see that I need help,
when I refuse to ask for the help I need.

Help me
to admit when my teaching is not effective,
or my classroom management is not working.
Lead me to ask others for advice.

Help me
to see when my students need more than I can give,
or their families need professional assistance.
Lead me to make appropriate referrals.

Help me
to acknowledge when I am too tired to do a good job,
or the flame of my passion for teaching has burnt out.
Lead me to find rest and renewal,
to care for myself so that I will be able to care for others.

God, who knows my every need,
help me to know what I need and to be willing to ask for it.
Amen.

Is This Another Fad?

Eternal God,
whose loving will is unchanging,
whose salvation is the sure foundation
on which my life is built,
when I feel buffeted by the gusty winds of educational reform,
help me to discern the truths that will stand for all time.

Education is constantly being reformed.
"The experts" keep revising their recommendations
about what to teach and how to teach it.
The experts disagree with each other.
The experts and the politicians disagree even more.

Sometimes it seems like
curriculum changes are effective responses to different times, and
instructional changes are creative ways to teach diverse students.
I celebrate and give thanks for such positive changes.

But sometimes it seems like
changes aren't really changes—
they are just new names for old truths.
And sometimes, unfortunately,
changes seem to be misguided—even reckless—
change for the sake of change, a fad,
change to promote a political agenda,
worst of all, change for the sake of someone's profit,
a bottom line that is commercial, not educational.
I deplore the waste and discord of such negative changes.

Eternal God,
give me grace to embrace positive changes—
even when they mean more work for me!
Give me courage to resist negative changes—
even when their allure is strong.
Give me wisdom to discern the difference,
to teach what matters in ways that work,
to stand with you on the rock of eternal truth.
Amen.

∞

To Be a Model

A teacher is a model.
Students learn from what I say,
and even more from what I do.

God, empower me.
By the grace of your redeeming love
revealed in Jesus the Christ, your Son,
the model of perfect obedience to your will,
may I be a model
of learning and working and living
who is in all things worthy of Christ's name.

May I model the love of learning:
actively seeking to expand my knowledge,
exploring and valuing others' points of view,
thinking deeply to increase my understanding,
living my commitment to lifelong learning.

May I model excellence in working:
striving to do my best,
learning from mistakes and failures,
persevering when challenged,
living my commitment to continuous improvement.

May I model compassion in living,
treating every person with respect and dignity,
demonstrating care and concern for people in need,
advocating for children and others without a voice,
living my commitment to justice and peace for all.

Jesus is my model.
I learn from the record of what he said,
and even more from what he did for me.
God, empower me to be a model for others,
in all things worthy of Christ's name. Amen.

Save Me from the Politics

God, you got me into this.
Help me to remember what I'm here for.

I'm teaching because:
I love learning.
I love to help others learn.
I learn from helping others learn.
I love the children who are my students.
I believe that all children have a right to learn.
I am committed to creating a better future
for our world, and
I believe that begins with educating children.

I am sometimes surprised, even bemused,
but more often frustrated and deeply concerned because
teaching and learning are not just educational issues
with decisions based upon educational research and expertise.
How we educate our children is a controversial political issue
with decisions based upon competition for power:
who has the most money, who shouts the loudest,

whose ideology prevails at any given time;
with decisions made in boardrooms and legislatures by politicians
who have little or no understanding
of the impact of their decisions.
Sometimes I accept and even appreciate,
other times I am compelled to fight against,
always I have to live with the decisions of such officials.

God, you got me into this.
Help me to remember what I'm here for.
Help me to stay focused on my students.
Help me to ignore the politics that threaten to distract me.
Help me to stay focused on my teaching
and my students' learning.
Help me to combat the politics that detract from either one—
     or both.

God, give me the wisdom and the power
to see and resist decisions that are about politics and power,
to see and celebrate decisions that help us
to better educate all children.
God, it is you
calling us to create a better future for your world
beginning with your children. Amen.

To Love Myself?

To love my neighbors as myself.
I understand the part about my neighbors.
I'm not sure what it means to love myself.

Teaching is a service profession,
a daily opportunity to give to others.
It can be challenging intellectually

to understand deeply and explain well
what I want my students to learn.
It can also be emotionally draining
to be present and responsive
to the variety of needs my students bring.

God, I accept your call to love my students.
They are my neighbors at school.
God, help me to understand that
to be of service, to give myself to them,
I have to have something to give.

To eat regularly and well.
To exercise and sleep enough.
To seek medical care when I need it.
God, help me to see and do what I need to do
to care for the body you have given me.

To nurture family members near and far.
To sustain meaningful relationships with friends.
To laugh and play and eat together.
To share the secrets of my soul and listen to theirs.
God, help me to see and do what I need to do
to care for the relationships you have given me.

To follow Jesus Christ and grow in faith.
To read the Bible and pray and listen for your word.
To study and worship with sisters and brothers in Christ.
God, help me to see and do what I need to do
to care for my spiritual life, the gift of your saving grace.

God, I accept your call to love myself.
With your help, I will see and do what I need to do.
Amen.

I'm Losing It

It's a cliché.
But it's true.
I am stressed out . . . burning out.
I am not eating right.
I am not sleeping well.
I am working hard,
but I feel like I'm spinning my wheels.
I can list all the things
I should be doing differently,
but I can't make myself do them.

Merciful God,
I lift myself to you
wholly
just as I am.

Rekindle my love of teaching.
Empower me to take better care
of the body you have given me.
Guide me to make better use
of the gifts you have given me.
Give me strength to do what I can do,
and courage to leave the rest to you.

Merciful God,
hear my prayer.
Amen.

Living within My Limits

Humbly I pray.

God, you know me. You made me. You love me. Limited as I am.

You know me better than I know myself.
You know my high aspirations, goals, and commitments:
my longing to make a real difference in the lives of my students,
my desire to be a supportive colleague and team member at school,
my pledge to participate in the worship and mission of my church,
my vow to be an advocate for all the children in our community,
even my wish to contribute time and money to all the good causes
that would promote the reign of your will on earth.

You know all that I want to do.
You also know better than I know the limits of what I can do.
You know how often I feel frustrated, guilty, or angry because
I am limited by the number of hours in a day, and days in a week,
by the knowledge and expertise that I have and don't have, and
by the resources available to me, energy and money as well as time.

You made me:
Human. Gifted. And limited.
Forgive me when I slip into thinking that I should be:
Superhuman. Unlimited. Divine?

God, you know me. You made me. You love me. Limited as I am.

Teach me to live at peace within my limits.
Teach me to know my limits and to accept them with grace
instead of frustration, guilt, and anger.

Help others to understand and accept my limits with grace.
Help me to understand and accept the limits of others with grace.
Keep us from imposing upon each other frustration, guilt, or anger.

God, teach me to live at peace within my limits.
Empower me to see and do all that I possibly can,
and to accept with grace all that I cannot. Amen.

5 ❀ Prayers for Students of All Ages

EARLY CHILDHOOD

Praise for the Miracle of Life

Almighty God,
Creator of the heavens and earth,
Giver of the life that springs from love,
all of creation reveals your glory;
all honor and praise be yours.

How great is the gift of human life.
How miraculous is the birth of a baby.
How sacred is her growth and development.
How precious is his trust in those who nurture him.
How joyful is her first smile.
How exciting is his first word.
How spectacular is her first step.
How unbelievably soon is his first day of school.

How great is the gift of human life.

How life-changing is the birth of a baby.
Giver of the life that springs from love,
all of creation reveals your glory;
all honor and praise be yours.
Amen.

Beginning with Babies

On the loveseat in my home office
there is a pillow given to me when my first child was born.
Embroidered on the pillow is this anonymous quote:
"A baby is God's opinion that the world should go on."

In the vastness of the universe,
yes, but also
in the tiny fingers of a newborn baby,
we see God's creative power.

Creator God, we thank you for babies.
Thank you for their incredible eagerness to learn about the world:
fingers outstretched to touch everything,
mouths open to taste everything that will fit,
eyes flashing back and forth to see everything,
ears turning heads to hear everything,
noses wrinkled to smell everything,
brains making infinite connections
as minds seek to make sense of everything.

Saving God, we pray for babies as they grow.
We pray that they will always have
parents who love them,
food that nourishes them,
clothing that warms them,
homes that shelter them,

doctors who care for them,
teachers who inspire them, and
communities of faith that nurture them.

Holy God, Spirit of Love moving among us,
teach us to love and care for the babies in our midst
that they might grow as Jesus did
in wisdom and in stature and in favor with you.
Amen.

Learning from Little Ones

Blessed are the babies.
They are God's gift of new life,
harbingers of hope.

Blessed are the toddlers.
They show us that learning to walk
sometimes requires holding on to others, and
sometimes means picking oneself up after a fall.

Blessed are the "terrible two"-year-olds.
They stomp and shout their independence,
an often frustrating, never subtle, reminder
of how important it is to find one's own voice.

Blessed are the three- and four-year-olds.
With hands that touch and draw and build,
with feet that run and climb and splash in puddles,
with minds eager to explore and understand,
they challenge us
to live with open hands and feet and minds,
to embrace the world,
to rejoice in the gift of life itself.

Thank you, God, for the blessing of young children.
Teach us to receive children as gifts of life and love.
Teach us to learn from them, lessons that come from you.
Teach us to love them, as you love them, as you have loved us
unconditionally . . . eternally.
In the name of Jesus,
who embraced the children,
Amen.

Firsts

I am Shandra's first school teacher.
Sammy is not potty trained yet.
Khalid has not learned how to take turns.
Alexa has never had to share her toys with other children.
Hassan still sits in the corner crying.
Eliot has never before used a pair of scissors.
This is the first time Ryan's mother has left him
with a group of strangers in a strange place.
Latisha is afraid that her mother won't come back.

I teach young children.
So often I am their first teacher.
My class is their first school experience.
My students are their first schoolmates.
What a privilege. What an awesome responsibility.

I love every one of them.
I want them to feel welcome and loved.
I want them to make friends.
I want them to learn and grow in so many ways.
I want them to succeed in school.
I want them to know they can succeed.

I want them to love learning.
I want them to believe in themselves.

O God, who is first in all things,
I can make their first experiences all that you intend.
But not alone. Only with your help.
God, give me strength and patience and wisdom.
God, give me colleagues and partners to work with.
God, give me love.
God, be with me. Now and always.
Amen.

Joy and Laughter

God of joy and laughter,
I rejoice to teach young children.
I laugh with delight for the gift of their presence in my life.

Thank you for their wonder
as they watch ducklings hatch in the incubator.
Thank you for the growing muscles
with which they climb the jungle gym.
Thank you for their enthusiasm
when they raise their hands to answer my question.
Thank you for the pride
with which they stand and share during show-and-tell time.
Thank you for the joy in their faces
when they learn to read their names.
Thank you for the laughter in their voices
when they tell a knock-knock joke.

Bountiful God, from whom all gifts come,
keep my heart open to receive the gifts of young children.
Keep my life open to be transformed by their joy and laughter.
Amen.

What Chance Do They Have?

God whose Spirit
is the breath of life itself,
God whose Son
welcomed the children in his arms,
God whose Love
embraces every newborn baby,
hear my desperate prayer
for every baby born
at the edge of life,
deprived of welcoming arms,
without human love.

Babies born
with fetal alcohol syndrome
addicted to crack
with the HIV virus
too small and too early
because of others' choices.
Babies living
without enough food
without adequate medical care
in squalor
without caregivers
who have the means and the knowledge
and the desire to care for them.

Babies born unwanted.
Babies living without love.
Children without a chance
long before they enter my classroom.
In human terms, the beginning is the end.

Spirit of Love revealed to us in the Son,
by his grace, we do not live in human terms.

I pray for the day when every baby will be wanted and loved,
and every child will have a chance to live as you intend.
I pray for the heart to love and teach and give every chance
to all the students in my class, whatever their beginnings.
Whatever the beginning, may the end be your will.
Amen.

CHILDHOOD

Developmentally Appropriate Practice

God, our Creator,
how magnificent is your creation of humankind.
How wondrous is the unfolding of each individual life.
Your love gives us birth.
Your Spirit guides our growth and development.

Each student who comes to school is an individual
whose path of growth and development is unique.
That means the children in my class are different from one another.
They come with different backgrounds and experiences.
Their hands are ready to hold pencils and use scissors
at different times.
They learn to read at different ages and different speeds.
Their minds grasp and remember new information
at different rates.
They even started school at different ages.

God who made and loves them all,
teach me to respect and appreciate all the individuals in my class.
Teach me to teach them
in ways that are developmentally appropriate,
being sensitive to their readiness,
challenging them just enough,
walking alongside to support and encourage them

whether they are learning fast or slow.
Teach me how to teach them
so that I may be an instrument of your Spirit,
guiding them to grow and develop as you desire.
Amen.

Reading, Writing, and Arithmetic

God incarnate,
Christ alive among us,
you walk beside us,
sharing our joys,
celebrating our accomplishments.

Hear this glad prayer
of praise and thanksgiving
for the thrill my students feel
when they master new skills and
experience success at school.

Hooray for learning
to recognize letters and read simple words,
to count to one hundred by ones and then tens,
to write the alphabet and spell one's own name,
to read from left to right aloud with expression,
to subtract from right to left, and regroup, too,
to write a sentence, and then a paragraph,
to memorize the times-tables and do long division,
to write in cursive and type on a keyboard,
to read chapter books and write book reports.

Hallelujah for learning
to read and write and do arithmetic,
tools for living, skills we need, whatever we do.

Hear this glad prayer
of praise and thanksgiving
for the happiness I feel
when my students learn new skills and
grow confident about their competence.
Hooray! Hallelujah!
Amen.

⬭

Teaching and Learning to Read

Letters and sounds. Phonemic awareness.
Helping young students to learn their letters,
to understand that letters have sounds,
to begin to decode the words
that are letters and sounds put together
is to give them the key
to unlock the mystery of printed symbols.

Thank you, God, for each child's effort,
head bowed over the book in concentration,
finger pointing to each word on the page,
breath-held pauses and soft, tentative sounds.
Thank you, God, for each child's achievement,
eyes shining and face grinning with pride as
each word is sounded out, each sentence read aloud.

Help me, God, to encourage each student's effort.
Help me, God, to persevere until each one succeeds.
Give me patience and an assortment of strategies
to assist those who struggle and learn to read more slowly.

When I consider the power of the written word
to open the mind to a vast world of ideas,
to evoke the deepest of human emotions,
to stir the spirit to seek truth and justice,

I am humbled by the privilege that is mine.
When I contemplate the necessity of reading
for success in school and society,
I am compelled to redouble my efforts
to meet the challenge for every child.

God who is the Word incarnate,
whose eternal love for humankind is recorded
in the written words of the Bible,
thank you for the privilege and the challenge,
the blessing of teaching children to read. Amen.

Tattletales

Mrs. B., he's hitting me.
Dr. K., she took my pencil.
Ms. R., he won't share.
Mr. D., she's not doing what you said.

In the primary grades
children are such tattletales.
I know that tattling is
a normal typical to-be-expected
behavior at this stage of their lives,
but sometimes it drives me crazy.
They are so eager to make sure
I know what every other child
is doing or not doing or should be doing.

God, you love them even when they are tattling.
God, you love me no matter how frustrated I feel.
Give me eyes to see and ears to hear
student behaviors that I need to know about.
Keep me cool and calm and able to ignore
student behaviors that I don't need to worry about.

Help me to model and teach my students
how to monitor their own behavior instead of others',
ways to resolve minor conflicts on their own, and
when to seek additional assistance from me.
Grant me the ability to discern those times
when I must intervene to protect a student from harm,
whether physical, emotional, or spiritual.

God, you place these students in my care.
Bless me with patience and wisdom
to know how to respond to whatever tales they tell.
Amen.

Multiple Gifts

God our Maker,
your creative power makes
every snowflake different,
every fingerprint unique.
Your loving wisdom makes
every human person a one-of-a-kind gem.
I teach a class of such gems.

You have given to each of them
a unique array of multiple gifts:
talents, abilities, intelligences,
strengths, capacities, potential.
Whatever the experts may call them,
I know they are gifts from you.
Thank you, God, for the multiple gifts
that each student brings to the class.

You have loved each of them individually.
Teach me, God, to do the same.
Forgive me when impatience or limited vision

keeps me from seeing the gifts a student brings.
Give me eyes that recognize and a heart that embraces
the gifts each and every one brings to the class.
Guide me to teach in ways that help students
to identify and develop their own gifts, and
to acknowledge and celebrate the gifts of others.

God who has given me the gifts and the call to teach,
help me to receive the students in my class
as beautiful gems to be polished and treasured,
as precious gifts that you have entrusted to my care.
Amen.

Beyond Gender Stereotypes

Created by God. In the image of God.
Male and female. God created us.

Thank you, God, for the girls and boys in my class.
Girls who giggle and girls who climb trees.
Boys who shout and boys who hug their dolls.
Girls who play dress-up and girls who hammer nails.
Boys who build towers and boys who write poems.
Girls who read well and girls who stand up to the boys.
Boys who excel in math and boys who are not afraid to cry.
Girls and boys. Individuals.
Individuals different in the way their bodies are created.
Individuals alike in the need to laugh and learn and be loved.
Individuals different in personalities, in their gifts, and
in the activities they want to do, if we allow them a choice.
Individuals alike in the right to explore their interests
and develop the many, varied talents you have given them.
Different and alike. Individuals all.

Thank you, God, for the girls and boys in my class.
Help me to move beyond gender stereotypes
to embrace them all as individuals,
whose needs I will seek to meet,
whose personalities I will respect,
whose abilities I will celebrate,
whose choices I will neither assume nor limit
on the basis of their gender.
Help me to move beyond gender stereotypes
to embrace each one as an individual,
determined as I am
to give every girl and boy every opportunity
to pursue unique interests with enthusiasm,
to develop special talents with passion.

Thank you, God, for the girls and boys in my class.
Help me to see that they are created in your image, and
to love them as you love them, individuals all. Amen.

On Their Own — Ready or Not

God who loves us with a parent's love,
God who adopts us as beloved children,
hear my prayer for young students
who go home to empty houses.

I am trying not to judge others' decisions.
I understand that there are many reasons
why a parent or caregiver is not present:
the need to work, no money for a sitter,
misperceptions of a child's maturity,
an apparent lack of options.

The elementary school years are a time of transition.
Rates of development are so variable.

Some days some students are ready and able
to be at home alone.
Some days the same students are not.
Some students are just not yet ready and able,
but still they are at home alone.

Loving God,
I pray that
you will watch over young students
who go home to empty houses.
I pray that
they will be safe and healthy,
they will use their time responsibly,
they will not be exposed to any of the many things
that could harm their minds or hearts or bodies.
I pray that
the students' parents and guardians
will find ways to provide the care their children need,
at home and in the world.
I pray that
you will use me as an instrument
of your loving care for children—whatever their need.
Amen.

Innocence Stolen

My heart aches.
He is seven and talking tough
like a teenage bully.
She is eight and wearing high heels
like a debutante.
They are nine and swinging their hips

in the sexually suggestive ways
they have seen on TV.
They are in elementary school
but they know or think they know
all about "sex, drugs, and rock 'n' roll."
Whatever they know, it is too much.

My heart aches
because I know, God,
it does not have to be this way.
I'm convinced, God,
you do not want it to be this way.

Merciful God, forgive us,
we who are the adults of this world,
for allowing a corrupt culture
to poison the minds and bodies of
the children of this world.
Forgive us
for giving them violent video games,
for dressing them up like adult dolls,
for surrounding them with a culture
that shouts sex at every turn.
Forgive us
for allowing children's eyes to see so much more
than their minds or hearts are ready to understand.

Merciful God, forgive me,
whenever and however I participate
in stealing the innocence of children.
Help me to see—and do—what I can
to change the world for children.
Amen.

ADOLESCENCE

On Fitting In

Cliques.
Oh, God, how I hate them.
I'm convinced
middle school is the hardest time of all for students.
They're not little kids. They're not grown up.
They want so much to fit in,
to dress and act and think like their peers
in order to be liked by their peers.
Instead of getting to know and appreciate one another,
they cling to best friends and cliques and crowds.
They tease and taunt and shut each other out.
It hurts me to see
how often and how deeply they keep hurting each other.
Please, God,
heal the pain that my students inflict upon each other.

God of infinite mercy,
you accept us just as we are,
and challenge us to accept each other.
God of limitless love,
you loved us so much that you sent Jesus
to show us how to live with love for one another.

God, my teacher and my guide,
use me as a vessel of your mercy and a model of your love.
Give me grace
to accept each of my students,
and to show them how to accept each other.
Give me love
to care for my students, and to unite them in an open community
characterized by mutual caring and respect.

Oh, God,
help me to end the cliques.
Amen.

Male and Female, You Created Us

Creator of the earth,
Maker of humankind,
how incredible to think
that you made us in your own image.
Thank you for the gift of the Spirit,
the holy breath that gives us life.
How awesome to ponder
that you created us, male and female,
alike and yet different.
Thank you for the gift of gender,
the mystery and the blessing
of being a man . . . of being a woman.

Designer of their development,
I pray for my middle school students
as they enter into that stage we call puberty.
All at their own times . . .
Fast and slow . . .
Girls before boys . . . mostly . . .
Budding breasts, fuzzy whiskers, long legs . . .
Raging hormones . . . so many changes.

God, who watches over all,
watch over my students as they grow and develop.
Help them to accept and respect and care for
their own changing bodies.
Help them to accept and respect and care for
their classmates whose bodies are changing, too.

As they struggle to discern
what it means for them to be young men and young women,
teach them to celebrate the ways
that you have made them alike . . . and different.
Help them to give thanks for the gift of their own gender.

God, who watches over me,
give me patience
and the wisdom to respond appropriately
to the needs of my middle school students
as they move through puberty.
Amen.

An Open Door

God of all wisdom, you know that
adolescence can be a stormy time.
There are students in my classes
whose pain I can glimpse:
who find it hard to learn,
who are unhappy with their bodies,
who have been hurt by classmates
and abandoned by adults,
who are uncertain and anxious
about what the future will hold.
There are other students in my class
struggling in ways I do not even know.

God of all love, you know that
the students in my classes need
an adult whom they can trust,
an adult who will listen,
an adult to talk to,
an adult who embodies your love for them.

God who is the source of wisdom and love in my life,
let me be that adult for my students.

Remind me
to keep open the door to my classroom.
Guide me
to keep open the doors of my mind and heart
to let students enter in.

Empower me to become
someone students can talk to,
someone they trust to listen and care.
Use me to make your love known to them.
Make me a channel of your grace.

In the name of Jesus the Christ,
who is your love incarnate. Amen.

Stop the Bullying

God in Christ,
who reconciles us to you, and
bids us make peace with one another,
I pray for peace and reconciliation
among the students in my school:
in classrooms, hallways, and cafeterias,
on playgrounds and school buses.

It saddens me to see
the way that some students shun others,
never choosing her for their team,
complaining when asked to be his partner,
making fun of what she said,
leaving him always to sit alone.
It grieves me to hear

their cruel words of ridicule and hatred,
"you're an idiot,"
"she's a nerd," "he's a [bleep],"
"get out . . . you don't belong here,"
and so much worse.
It makes me cringe within
to see one student strike another's body,
to hear about violence and threats of violence
that keep some students living in fear.

God who loves all and wills that we live in peace,
I believe your heart is breaking, too.

Hear my prayer: stop the bullying.
Heal the wounded spirits and minds and bodies
of those who have been bullied,
and those who have been the bullies.
Restore relationships that are broken;
build community where there was none.

Hear my prayer: use me to help stop the bullying.
Fill me with the power of your love,
so that I can be a peacemaker within the school.
Fill me with the gift of your peace,
so that I can be a minister of reconciliation. Amen.

∞

Living the Questions

Savior God,
who offers us the gift of grace
and gives us the gift of freedom to accept it or not,
Patient God,
who embraces us when we say,
"I believe. Help my unbelief":

Hear my prayer
for students who are struggling to figure out
what they believe.

They are asking important questions.
"Who am I?
What is important in my life?
What are the values I will live by?
What do I think about religion? politics? love? work?
Is there a God? How do we know?
What difference does it make?"

Help them to feel your love
sustaining them even as they wrestle with hard questions.
Help them to hear your Word,
guiding them to find faithful answers.
Help them to accept your saving grace
leading them to lives of purpose and joy.

God whose power is present
in the questions as well as the answers,
hear my prayer
for students who are struggling to figure out
what they believe.
Amen.

At Risk

O God who fashioned the stages of our growth,
O God who loves us in every stage,
I pray for my students as they navigate
this stage of development we call adolescence.

Especially I pray for those whose actions
put themselves and others at risk.

Perhaps it is because
they think they are invulnerable, or
they have succumbed to the temptations
that surround them at every turn, or
they are desperate to be accepted
by a group of their peers, or
they have not been respected and
so do not know how to respect themselves.
Whatever the reasons for their choices,
I am afraid for them. I pray for them.

I pray for students
who start to smoke at age thirteen,
who are drinking at age fifteen,
who drive too fast and jump off cliffs,
who stop going to school,
who experiment with drugs,
who are children bearing children.
I pray for those I can name . . .
and those I don't know,
for all students whose behaviors
destroy bodies, shut down minds, break hearts.

I pray that they will find
a reason and a way
and people who will help them
to make different choices.
I pray that they will repent,
which means to stop and turn around
and live life in a new way.
I pray that they will find your way for them.
Until then, I pray simply
that they will be safe. Amen.

What Do You Mean, You Have Other Things to Do?

Thank you, God!!
I love teaching high school.
I get to specialize,
to teach the discipline that I love most.
It feels so good
to believe in what I'm doing,
to be genuinely excited about the curriculum,
to inspire students with my own enthusiasm.

Forgive me, God,
when I get carried away,
when I act as if my class
is the only one that matters,
when I fail to be sensitive
to the many demands on students.

Remind me to listen, God,
when students come to me anxious
because of all that they have to do.

Empower me to respond, God,
in ways that are appropriate:
respectful of their time and varied needs,
fair and flexible as circumstances may require,
yet resisting the temptation to give up
and make life easy for them.

Challenge me, God, to teach always
in ways that are both fair and challenging:
inspiring, encouraging, and enabling my students
to do and learn as much as they possibly can,
to discover and grow into the life you desire for them.

It is you, O God, who inspires and enables me
to live into the fullness of life in Jesus Christ. Amen.

The Search for Identity

Creator of the heavens and earth,
Designer of day and night,
Keeper of the rhythm of the seasons,
Guardian of humankind
through all the seasons of our lives:
How magnificent are the works of your hands.
How marvelous is the process of human development.

You created every girl and boy I teach.
You have made each one unique:
blessed with different abilities,
motivated by diverse possibilities, and
shaped by varied experiences.

As a high school teacher, I watch them
seeking to discern their unique identities:
discovering their potential,
exploring options for their lives, and
striving to understand their experiences.

You love every girl and boy I teach.
You invite them to find their identities in you:
to appreciate and develop the gifts you have given them,
to pursue their interests with passion for others, and
to experience the gift of your amazing grace.

As a high school teacher, I pray for them
that they might accept your invitation:
using their talents in service to others,
choosing paths of justice and righteousness,
living with grace, growing in faith through every experience.

God who created my students,
God who created me:
I have accepted your invitation.

Help me to use my gifts to serve others as a teacher.
Guide me along paths of justice and righteousness
Empower me to live with grace and grow in faith each day,
that my life and identity might be a model for my students.
Amen.

To Choose Their Own Paths

What should she be when she grows up?
What should he do with his life?
These are essential questions
about vocations and values,
decisions that young women and men
must make for themselves.

God who created each one,
I pray for my students
that they will not just do
what others want them to do,
however well-intentioned
the wishes of parents
or grandparents or friends.
I pray for my students,
that, led by your Spirit,
they will honestly appraise
their abilities and interests,
and fully explore
all the possibilities before them.
I pray for my students,
that, led by your Spirit,
they will choose their own paths.

God who created each one
and made them all unique,

remind all of us
who love these young people
that what they should do
is for them to decide,
led, we pray, by
the wisdom and power
of your holy, loving Spirit.
Amen.

For Adolescent Girls

God of all, I pray for adolescent girls.
I've read the research. I've seen it happen.
Sometimes, as girls move into adolescence,
they lose their voices and give up their dreams.
Some girls cease to speak up in class,
to assert their points of view out of fear
of appearing unfeminine or not being liked by boys.
Others excel but don't take advanced courses or
pursue careers in science or computers or math,
at best, simply because no one encourages them,
at worst, because someone actively discourages them.
There are girls working toward college and careers.
Others want families, not careers; "work" is a transition stage.
Some want to believe they can have it all, but don't know how.
I know there is not one right way for all girls.
But, God, I really thought it would be easier by now,
for each girl to claim her gifts and find her own way.

God of all, I pray
for adolescent girls as they chart their paths through the confusion,
for high school teachers and school leaders who work with them,
for the community and world into which we send them.

Give to all girls: wisdom and courage and persistence
to identify the talents you have given them and
to choose their futures,
to pursue the vocations to which you call them,
whatever they may be.

Give to all of us who work with them:
humility and open minds and courage
to acknowledge our prejudices, enlarge our vision, and assist them
as they explore their abilities and options and
make their own decisions.

Give to the community and beyond: the will and the resources
to build a society in which all girls and boys, women and men,
can discover the gifts you have given and the life
to which you call them.

In the name of Jesus Christ,
who with perfect freedom lived
in perfect obedience to your will.
Amen.

Signs of Deep Distress?

How do I know, God,
if crying in the hallway
is a sign of depression
or a fleeting boyfriend crisis?
How do I know, God,
when acting out in class
suggests a serious emotional disturbance
rather than confusion or boredom?
How do I know, God,

if complaints about life at home
are indicators of severe dysfunction
or a teenager's healthy rebellion?

I'm not a mental health expert.
How do I know, God,
when "problems" are a phase
that a student will grow through, and
when they are evidence of
a student's need for professional help?

God who wills to work through me,
help me to learn all that I can
about the struggles of adolescence.
Help me to be there for my students,
a supportive presence to whom they can turn.
Help me to look and listen for signs of distress
suggesting their pain is more than a phase.
Help me to know when I cannot meet their needs
and must turn to those with greater expertise.
Help us all to know when we must intervene
to protect a student from self or others.

God who knows what I do not,
give me wisdom to know what I need to know
to respond sensitively and appropriately
to students' ambiguous messages.
Tune my heart to hear their cries for help.
Amen.

What Will They Do Next?

The end of high school.
Commencement.
The beginning of the next stage.
What will it be?

Seniors preparing to graduate.
It is time for them to decide.
What will they do next?

God who is present always
to love and comfort us through every ending,
to love and lead us into every beginning,
you know their hearts and minds;
you know their abilities and needs.
Guide them in this time of transition.

Some are ready and eager to go away to college.
Others want to begin at the local community college.
Some will enter school-to-work transition programs.
Others have already signed up for military service.
Some will be apprentices learning a skilled trade.
Others seek entry-level jobs from which to advance.
Some have the luxury of taking time for global travel.
Others face the necessity of work to pay for tuition.

Some know what they want to do and are ready to do it.
Others don't know and need time set aside to figure it out.

God who is present always,
guide these seniors, soon-to-be graduates, young adults.
Guide them as they decide what to do next.
Guide them through the ending of high school.
Guide them into the beginning of their futures,
wherever and whatever they may be.
Guide them in and through this time of transition. Amen.

College Letters

Another request.
Would I please write a letter of reference
and send it to these two or five or ten colleges
by this or that deadline?

Writing college recommendations.
One of many things they didn't tell me about
when I was a student
learning to be a high school teacher.
It's a chore. It's a privilege.
It is an opportunity to make a difference.

Dear God,
I am sitting at my desk
staring at the computer screen.
What can I say about this student?
I take this responsibility very seriously.
I want to be both honest and generous,
to write enthusiastically about her strengths.
I want to be an effective advocate,
to highlight something special or unique
so that his file will receive a fair review.
It's December. A crazy, busy time.
I want to be dependable
to find time to do a good job on time.

God above, who knows and sees all,
help me to recognize and rejoice in the gifts
that make each student unique and special.
God on earth, speaking through human voices,
help me to find the words to convey to others
what each one offers to a college community.
God within me, make me an instrument of your grace.
Help me to fulfill this responsibility with integrity.
God, here at my desk, guide my words. Amen.

Children Having Children

Thirteen and pregnant.
Seventeen and pregnant for the second time.
Fifteen and pregnant and she has a toddler at home.
Eighteen and pregnant and she has AIDS.

God who created us male and female,
God who gives us the gift of sexuality,
I wish teenagers weren't having sex.
I wish adolescent girls were not becoming pregnant.
I wish children did not have children to raise.
But I cannot make my wishes come true.

I am a high school teacher and every year
teachers and counselors and administrators
must teach and guide and seek to love and care for
teenagers who are pregnant.

I pray for all girls and boys that they will wait.
I pray for the girls and boys who do not wait
that they will take responsibility
to protect themselves from pregnancy and disease.
I pray for girls who become pregnant
and for the boys who "get them" pregnant
that they will seek help and make wise choices.
I pray for girls and boys and their families
whatever their choices
because I know they are never easy choices.

I pray for myself and for all adults
who work with teenagers,
chaste and sexually active, pregnant and not.
I pray that by your grace
we will love and forgive and accept each one
as you have loved and forgiven and accepted us.
I pray that by your grace

we will help them to make good decisions.
I pray that by your grace
we ourselves will be positive role models
of sexuality, of responsibility, of wisdom,
of your loving will for all. Amen.

Choosing a College

Small college in the city?
Large university in a rural setting?
County community college?
Professional training school?
Private college in the northeast?
State university in the South?
Girls' school? Religious school?
Liberal arts degree? A major in?
To live at school? Or, at home?
The alternatives are countless,
the costs staggering, and
the decisions life-changing.

God who gives us choices
and guides our decision-making
if we ask and listen,
hear my prayer for high school seniors
who are going to college
and for their parents as together
they collect information and visit and
contemplate college possibilities.

My prayer for them is simply this:
They will have the information they need,
understanding of themselves and their options.
They will take time to reflect carefully and,

led by your Spirit, make the best decisions possible.
They will find acceptance and the means
to live out the decisions they have made.

My prayer for school leaders, including myself,
is that we will support them through the process:
We will assist them in gathering information.
We will make time to listen and reflect with them.
We will advocate for them in letters and calls.
We will pray for them continually:
for good decisions, for acceptance, and yes, God,
for every opportunity to make their dreams come true.
Amen.

The Problem with Proms

O God. It's that time of year.
The junior prom. The senior prom.
As I watch and listen to a new group of students
preparing for these annual rituals of celebration,
you know I feel more anxious than happy.

I am dismayed by the excesses of some,
the number of dollars spent
on gowns and tuxedos and limousines and more.
I am frustrated by the inordinate emphasis
on asking and being asked and going to the prom
that excludes girls and boys
reluctant to attend because they don't have a date, or
unable to attend because they don't have the means.
I am concerned because
our culture has so glamorized drinking and sex
that some students want—even expect—both
to be part of their prom experience.

I am angry because I know there are parents
who provide the alcohol and hotel rooms.
I fear for my students' health and safety.

Steadfast God, you are present at all times and places.
Merciful God, may your presence at this time of year
guide all of the adults who influence and supervise students,
and protect all of the girls and boys who attend a prom.

May the attitudes and behaviors of adults
help students keep these events in perspective;
they are special times to be treasured, not abused.
May our policies and practices ensure that
proms are affordable and welcoming to all,
limits set by the school and the law are enforced,
and all students' well-being is safeguarded.
May we come together,
parents, teachers, principals, and chaperones,
limousine drivers and police officers,
to make the proms this year wonderful celebrations,
full of the kind of fun students will remember with joy
and never have to regret. Amen.

Commencement

I'm sitting
in the auditorium.
The speeches are over.
Finally.
I'm watching students
walk across the platform
in shorts and sandals
beneath caps and gowns
shaking hands

receiving diplomas
waving high-fives
to the shouts of friends
and family.
I'm watching parents
applauding
snapping photographs
amazed and misty-eyed.
Students and parents.
Struggling to let go.
Thrilled to have made it.
Eager to move on.
Laughing. Crying.
Exchanging hugs.
Sharing their pride.

As each name is called,
God, I lift a silent prayer.
Thank you for this young woman.
Watch over this young man.
God, bless each and every one
as they bid us farewell
and commence
the next stage of their lives.
Amen.

6 ✸ Prayers for Students with Special Needs

STUDENTS LIVING IN POVERTY

Poverty Kills

God of children who are poor, outcast, abandoned,
we confess our sin.

We know that
poverty destroys the bodies of children
who are born prematurely,
who do not receive medical care,
who are born with drug addictions,
who do not have enough food.

We know that
poverty destroys the minds of children
who are poisoned by lead,
who do not have enough food,
who never hear a story read,
who instead hear "you don't have a chance."

We know that
poverty destroys the spirits of children
who are not safe in their homes,
who attend failing schools,
who do not pass the high-stakes tests,
who do not believe they will live to adulthood.

God of children who are poor, outcast, abandoned,
we confess our sin.
We tolerate poverty. We accept its destruction.
We allow poverty to continue to destroy
the bodies, minds, and spirits
of the children whom you have set in our midst.

Merciful God,
forgive us.
Amen.

∞

The Achievement Gap

God of the poor and oppressed,
God of justice and righteousness for all,
with sad and repentant hearts,
faithful Christians must confess the many injustices
that persist in our time.
With sorrow and a plea for help,
Christian teachers are called to confront
the great inequity in education:
the achievement gap between students
who are poor and rich,
who live in cities and suburbs,
who are Caucasian and African-American,
Caucasian and Hispanic.

It's a huge problem
tackled but not solved by hundreds of experts.
I know that I can't do what they haven't done.
I cannot change the world all by myself.
But with your help, God, I can make a difference.
Give me eyes to see, and the will to do, what I can.

Within the context of my class,
never let me lower my expectations for a student
because she is poor, or because his skin is brown.
Help me to see the fullness of each child's potential,
to help every one reach the highest levels of learning.
Within my school and district,
make me a strong leader, insisting and ensuring
that all teachers learn what is required
to effectively teach children of every race and language.
Within my community and state,
at public meetings, through letters, and in the voting booth,
use me to advocate for changes and strategies proven to work.
Within my church,
lead me to join with others in the larger mission
of ending the injustice of poverty,
the source and fuel for so many inequities.

At every level of my life,
God, make me an instrument of your justice and righteousness.
With your help, I can make a difference.
Acting through your people, you can change the world. Amen.

The Neighborhood

This is where my students live.
This is what they see.
Houses boarded up. Abandoned. Crack houses.
Yards full of discarded junk. Overgrown lawns. Weeds.

Sidewalks littered with broken bottles. Used needles.
Street corner meetings of drug dealers and their customers.

This is what they hear.
Television. Boom boxes.
Tires squealing.
Drive-by shootings.
Police sirens.

God of children in this neighborhood,
why have we forsaken them?
How have we allowed this to happen?
When will it end?

God of children in this neighborhood,
I know all too well what I cannot do.
I cannot change the neighborhood.
I cannot protect them from its sights and sounds.

God of children in this neighborhood,
give me vision and give me hope.
Help me to see what I can do.
Help me to know how I can make a difference.
Give me courage and perseverance.
Help me to do what I can do. Amen.

The Temptation to Pity

God who knows the truths of my heart
even when I am unable to put them into words,
accept my confessions and confusion,
this humble plea for divine guidance.

Looking out from my middle-class suburban home,
it is easy to ignore the poverty

hidden within my community.
Looking out the windows of my urban classroom,
it is impossible to ignore the poverty
of the neighborhood where my students live.

I confess I am saddened
by some of the conditions I see on the street.
I confess I am angered
by some of the behavior I deal with in the classroom.
I confess I am appalled
by some of the stories I hear, true or not.

God of mercy, I also confess
my tendency to become patronizing,
to look down on parents whose lives I can't imagine,
to feel sorry for their children.
God of mercy, save me
from the temptation to feel sorry for my students.
I know they do not need my pity.
But I do not always know what they do need
or how to give it to them.

God who knows the truths of others' lives,
guide the response of my mind and heart
as I teach and work with students and families
whose lives are very different from my own.
Increase my understanding; deepen my respect.
Give me wisdom that sees my students' strengths;
give me love, a heart full of hope for each one.
Give me wisdom that knows what my students need;
give me love, a heart overflowing,
ready and able to meet their needs each day.
Amen.

A Dangerous Place

Merciful God,
what a privilege to confess to you
all that troubles my heart and mind.
What a gift is the promise of grace
that you will forgive what I repent,
that you will ease the burdens I bear.

I teach in a dangerous neighborhood.
Last year there were more murders here
than anywhere else in the city.
I love my students and this school, and
believe that you have called me to be here.
But I confess sometimes I am just plain scared.
What if I am in the wrong place at the wrong time?

Patient God,
who sees the big picture so much better
than I am ever able to do,
forgive me for giving in to the temptation
to focus on myself.
Put my concerns into perspective:
I go home to a safer place;
my students do not get to leave.
Hear my prayers for my students,
for the school, and for this neighborhood.

Watchful God,
protect the children of this neighborhood
as they travel to and from school,
as they walk to a store or try to play together.
Safeguard the students and teachers
who come to this school building each day,
that it might be a safe haven for all.
Work through parents and police officers,

community volunteers and political leaders
to transform this neighborhood into a
violence-free zone, a place of peace
in which children and adults can live and grow.
In the name of the Prince of Peace.
Amen.

STUDENTS OF DIVERSE CULTURES AND FAITHS

A Welcoming Home

A house is a building.
A home is a place where people
are connected to one another,
care for each other, and
learn and grow together.
A home is a place where every person
feels welcomed . . . and loved.

God, who connects and cares for us,
God, who nurtures our learning and growth,
hear my prayer.
Help me to make
the "house" of my classroom
into a home for my students.

What a wonderfully diverse group we are:
a symphony of different languages,
a congregation of many faiths,
a splendid multicolored tapestry
of race, ethnicity, and nationality.

God, who created us all to be different,
God, who loves us all the same,
hear my prayer.

Help me to accept each student in the class,
to model an open heart and mind for all.
Help me to value the unique gifts each student brings,
to model respect and appreciation for all.
Help me to create a space where
students and teacher alike are connected to one another,
care for each other, and learn and grow together.
Help me to model for others the love you have shown to me.

Help me to make my classroom
into a home for my students,
a place where each and every one
feels welcomed and loved.
Because you first welcomed and loved us.
Amen.

If I Am Honest with Myself

Merciful God, slow to anger and abounding in steadfast love,
Merciful God, who does not deal with us according to our sin,
hear my confession . . . honest, painful words.

Cultural pluralism. The nation is still growing and changing.
Cultural diversity. My classroom is changing, too.
Faces, hair, skin color, clothing. Languages, religions, values.
What to eat, how to communicate, when to celebrate.
There are many differences among us. Real differences.

If I am honest with myself,
I must confess the anxiety I sometimes feel
about teaching students whose lives are so different from my own.
I feel anxious about the changes I see
in my country and in my class.

There is much that is new . . . unfamiliar . . . unknown.
Culture shock, I guess they call it. I'm not prepared.

If I am honest with myself,
I must confess the anger and arrogance I sometimes feel
about teaching students whose lives are so different from my own.
I resent hearing that I have to make changes in the way I teach.
Why should I have to change anyway? Why can't they change?
Our culture . . . our ways of doing things are better. Aren't they?

Merciful God,
when I am honest with myself, I tell you what you already know.
Anxiety and anger and arrogance are a part of me.
Forgive me. Teach me to forgive and accept myself.
But do not stop there.

Replace my anxiety about changes in this nation
with enthusiasm for learning about its increasingly diverse cultures.
Turn the energy of my anger at having to make changes
in my classroom
into a passionate quest to understand and reach all my students.
Overcome my cultural arrogance with humility of mind and heart,
an openness—no, God, a commitment—
to respect and value all that I can learn
from those whose lives are so different from my own.
Because you are the One who made us all. Amen.

Culturally Responsive Teaching

Keishon learned that to look adults in the face
would be disrespectful.
Alicia learned to be casual about time
because her parents value time differently.
She is often late to class.
Dakota learned to put the needs of her group

before individual achievement.
She doesn't understand the concept of cheating
because she only knows how to work together.

How we look at each other,
and view time,
our goals for success.
Behaviors and values that are learned,
examples of our cultural differences.

Culturally responsive teaching.
It sounds complicated, perhaps even trendy.
Sometimes I want to resist it
because it sounds like more work,
or, more honestly,
because it may threaten
the behaviors and values that I have learned.

God, forgive my resistance.
I know that culturally responsive teaching is really
about meeting the needs of every student in my class
and teaching them all
to live and learn together in the classroom
so that they will be well prepared
to live and work together in a culturally diverse world.

God, guide my response.
I want to welcome students of every culture,
to receive those whose culture is different
from mine and classmates'
as an opportunity
to better understand the spectacular diversity of humankind,
to equip young people to build a world that embraces its diversity.
Thank you, God. It is an opportunity, and a gift.
Teach me to teach others in ways that are culturally responsive.
Amen.

Racism Is Real

"Jesus loves the little children, all the children of the world.
Red and yellow, black and white, they are precious in his sight,
Jesus loves the little children of the world."

It's true, Jesus. You love every child of every color.
It's also true that we fail to love children of every color.
Racism is real.

It's often unconscious, but not always.
Too many teachers still have low expectations
for the academic achievement of black students.
Too many cafeterias are still segregated,
with black students sitting apart from white classmates.
Too many administrators still look suspiciously
at the group of black boys hanging out in the hall.
Too many school activities still reflect our stereotypes:
black athletes and white science fair winners.

Hear my anguish, God, heal my heart.
I don't want to be racist, and I don't believe I am.
But I know that I am racist in ways I don't realize.
And I know that I am part of a world
that allows racism to continue
unseen, except perhaps by those who bear its burden,
unchecked by even the most well-intentioned Christians.

Lead me, God, to see and change what I can.
Guide me as a person.
May all my actions and attitudes reflect your love.
Guide me as a teacher.
May my class become a true community of learners
whose relationships cross the racial divide,
who strive together to meet my high expectations for all.
Guide me as an advocate for children of every color.
In the classroom and hallway, principal's office and boardroom,

at the street corner, church meeting, and ballot box,
may my eyes be open to recognize every evidence of racism,
may my voice be ready to speak loudly and clearly for every child.
Guide me as a follower of Jesus Christ who loves all the children.
May I be found faithful to him in my love for them. Amen.

English Language Learners

The Tower of Babel.
Confusion and misunderstanding.
The miracle of Pentecost.
Communication and understanding.

God in Christ Jesus,
the Word made flesh,
God in the Holy Spirit
that brought understanding
on the day of Pentecost,
hear my prayer.
By the power of your Word and Spirit,
bring understanding to my class.

The names and nations
have changed from year to year
but my class often includes
students learning English.
Jose was from Puerto Rico.
Pedro is from Cuba.
Bianca was from Mexico.
They all speak Spanish,
but not always in the same way.
Luiz was from Brazil
Etienne is from Senegal.
Keiko was from Japan.

They have all learned English,
but not at the same rate.

Thank you, God, for the gift of students
who speak languages other than English.
Forgive me, God, for being impatient
when I cannot understand them
and they cannot understand me.
Show me, God, how to communicate,
how to teach, and how to learn from them.
Use me, God, to teach all of my students
to appreciate and learn from each other.
By the power of your Word and Spirit,
bring understanding to my class. Amen.

One God Revealed in Many Ways

YHWH, God of the covenant with Abraham,
Allah, God revealed to Muhammad,
Triune God, Creator, Son, and Holy Spirit,
you are One.

You have revealed yourself throughout human history
in mighty acts of power and loving acts of grace,
in sacred words, whispered, shouted, written for all to read,
in song and dance and spirit-filled silence.
You have revealed yourself in many ways, but
you are One.

You revealed yourself to me through Jesus the Christ,
the Son you sent to save the world,
my teacher, my friend, my savior.
You are still revealing yourself to me
through the Bible and through prayer,

in worship and the fellowship of believers at church,
through acts of devotion and service.
You have loved me,
and made your love known to me,
and because of your love, I can love others.
Loving God, because of your love,
I can love others who know you in other ways.
You are One.

I do not claim to understand
the mysteries of the universe or
all the ways you choose to reveal yourself
to the people whom you have created, but
Loving God,
I know that you love the students in my class . . . all of them.
Loving God, so fill me with your love
that I too can love them,
that by my love for them
your love might be revealed.

YHWH, Allah, Creator, Son, and Holy Spirit,
you are One.
All thanks and praise, all honor and glory are yours. Amen.

STUDENTS WITH SPECIAL ABILITIES AND DISABILITIES

Seeing Abilities Instead of Disabilities

Able to paint beautiful pictures
using feet instead of hands.
Able to conduct leading scientific research
sitting in a wheelchair.
Able to communicate through a computer
without speaking a sound.

Able to bring people together,
but not to live independently.
Able to bring smiles to faces of all ages
and touch hearts at the deepest levels,
yet never to learn to read or write.

God whose creative love we know so surely:
You created every human body.
You fashioned the workings of every mind.
You breathed life into every human spirit.
God whose wisdom is beyond our knowing:
It is not ours to judge, nor to understand
why some have abilities that appear to be unlimited
and others have abilities that are profoundly limited,
and most of us fall somewhere in between.
Let it be for us enough to know
that you create each one and love us all.

In all my planning and teaching,
in every interaction with the students in my class,
may your creative, wise love work through me
to create a community of learners
in which the abilities of all
are nurtured to their fullest potential,
in which the disabilities of all
are accommodated with dignity and fairness,
in which the uniqueness of each one
is respected and valued by all.

God whose love is unlimited,
help me to see others with your eyes.
When I look at my students,
may I always see their abilities
before their disabilities. Amen.

High Standards for All

It's the law. Students with disabilities
will be in class with their nondisabled peers,
will have access to the general education curriculum,
will take the same high-stakes tests of achievement, and
will be held to the same learning standards as their peers
as much as is possible.
Exceptions have to be justified.

God whose perfect love
works through our imperfect human systems,
I support these high expectations,
and accept them as a challenge.

Whether I am teaching special education students
in a general education class, or a resource room,
with the help of push-in services, or pull-out programs,
co-teaching, or serving as a consultant teacher,
wherever and however
I am called to teach students with special needs
bless me, God, with what I need to meet the challenge.

Author of all wisdom, I need to know more.
Help me to find the time and resources and colleagues
to learn about a student's diagnosis and classification,
to understand his particular abilities and disabilities.

Teacher of amazing grace, I need to be able to do more.
Give me time and patience and a mind that is open
to learn prescriptive teaching strategies that will enable me
to implement her IEP and challenge her to learn to the fullest.

Spirit of infinite love, I need to be more loving.
Empower me to be a model of respect and appreciation,
to create a classroom of acceptance and cooperation
so that all students will meet high standards for learning,
and they will grow in spirit, the spirit of your love. Amen.

Before the Committee Meeting

Today's the day, God.
The Committee on Special Education is meeting.
Teachers and parents,
school staff and outside specialists,
diagnosticians and service providers—
they are all meeting together to decide about
the classification of students for special education,
the placement of students along a continuum of possible settings,
the accommodations and modifications, and related services
that students will need to succeed in school.

What an awesome responsibility, God.
To review all the information about each individual student,
to figure out where and how to help each one learn
as much as possible.

Spirit of God,
guide the discussion and the decisions.
Give to all who are present
ears that listen,
minds that reflect,
hearts that understand,
lips that speak words of truth in love.

Spirit of God,
use these people and this very human process
as an instrument of your holy will
for the students whom they serve.

Spirit of God,
when it is my turn to serve on this committee,
use me as an instrument of your holy will
for the students whom I will serve. Amen.

My First Inclusive Class

Mighty God,
Source of my life,
Spirit in whom I live and move and have my being,
walk beside me, please, to guide and strengthen me
as I face a new challenge.

This is a first for me.
My class this year will include several students with disabilities,
some mild, some severe.

I confess that I'm anxious and uncertain.
I don't know enough about their learning problems.
I am not sure how to handle their behavior problems.
I am not familiar with all the terms and requirements of their IEPs.
I never learned much about accommodations and modifications.
I admit I have mixed feelings about the whole idea of inclusion.
There will be a special education teacher in the class
some of the time.
I'm ambivalent about that, too. Will we be able to work together?

Merciful God,
forgive my fear of change; overcome my hardness of heart.
Replace my anxiety and ambivalence with hope and confidence.
Show me the way to make this work. Give me the courage to do it.
Help me to work with students and parents and other teachers
to create a classroom community
in which all students value and care for one another,
in which all students can learn to their fullest potential.
Help me to see this challenge as an opportunity for me to learn.

Mighty, merciful God,
Use me where I am . . . in this inclusive class
to teach all students . . . whatever their abilities and disabilities.
For you are the source of all life,
the Spirit in whom we all live and move and have our being.
Amen.

What's in a Label?

In the world of special education,
we are often forced to use labels.
For some students to receive what
they need to achieve in school,
we have to assess and diagnosis
and give their learning problems a name.
Names have power.

Forgive us, God, for the times
when the label name that we give to a student
is used to hurt that student and hinder success.
Forgive us, God, for identifying labels
that cause a student to be isolated or rejected,
that allow parents and teachers to give up on a student.

Thank you, God, for the times
when the label name that we give to a student
has the power to help that student succeed.
Thank you, God, for identifying labels that
help parents and teachers and other students
to understand and care for and teach each student.

God of all,
whose name is above all names,
who is the Word that saves humankind,
forgive us for misusing words in ways that hurt.
Teach us to use words in ways that help and heal.
In your name, and by your saving power.
Amen.

May I Please Have Your Attention?

Attention.
It's so important to learning.
In order for my students
to understand what I am saying,
to focus on what is most important,
to take good notes during the lesson,
to follow the problem-solving procedures
that I have demonstrated,
even to imitate the positive behaviors
of parents and teachers and peers;
in order for my students
to hear and see and understand
and remember new information,
they have to be able to pay attention.

God of all students,
who pays attention to their every need,
hear my prayer for the students in my class
who find it so hard—sometimes impossible—
to pay attention.
May the soothing breath of your Holy Spirit
calm their restless bodies, and quiet their racing minds.

God of all parents and professionals,
who pays attention to their every need,
hear my prayer for the people
who care for these students and seek to help them.
May the guiding love of your Holy Spirit
give them patience and understanding, and
inform their decisions about diagnoses and treatment plans.

God of all teachers,
who pays attention to our every need,
hear this humble prayer for myself.

May the wise counsel of your Holy Spirit
teach me how best to teach
each student with an attention problem.
Show me the way and give me the power, O Lord,
to help them to be able to pay attention
and learn about the wonders of your world. Amen.

Gifted and Talented

Amazing God,
who bestows on all individuals
special gifts and unique talents,
accept this prayer for myself and others
when I am called to teach
those students whose gifts and talents
are amazing, simply extraordinary.

It has been a rare privilege to know them.
Sue was four and reading sixth grade books.
Khalil was eight and composing music.
Maria was eleven and studying calculus.
Aaron was fourteen when he entered college.

It is a real challenge to teach them.
Ben already writes so eloquently.
Elaine solves logic problems I still can't get.
Lin knows more about the planets than I will ever know.
Sophia's voice is beautiful beyond words.
They are so far ahead of their peers, and sometimes me.
It's hard to keep up, to know what to do.
What more is there for me to teach them?

When I am privileged and challenged
to teach students with such awesome abilities:

help me to welcome them into my class
with wonder and thanksgiving;
help me not to be intimidated or annoyed
by their special gifts and needs.
Give me creativity and insight
to discover ways to keep them engaged and learning,
growing in areas of weakness as well as strength.
Give me patience and love
to overcome their frustrations as well as my own,
to integrate them fully in the community of their peers.

Amazing God,
use me and the special talents that you have given me
to be an effective teacher for all students,
including those who are called "gifted and talented." Amen.

Eighteen to Twenty-one

Depending on their needs,
students with disabilities are entitled
to receive special education services
until they are twenty-one years old.

These are transition years in which
to continue to develop the living skills
needed for adulthood,
at whatever level of independence
they will be able to achieve.

God of all, these are your children,
young adults with special needs.
I pray for them
that they will be empowered
to be lifelong learners,

to reach the fullness of their potential.
I pray for myself and all of us
who teach them,
that we will facilitate their learning,
that we will love them just as they are, and
nurture them toward all that they can be.
I pray for the communities
in which they will live,
that—regardless of the setting—
they will receive assistance and services as needed,
but most of all,
that they will be welcomed and integrated,
valued for their unique contributions.
I pray for them
that they will learn to be advocates for themselves,
visible and insistent
that they are your children too.

God in Christ, who gathered the children to himself,
fill our hearts and open our arms.
Teach us to love and embrace all your children
with the same welcoming arms you extend to them. Amen.

∞

STUDENTS WHO HAVE EXPERIENCED TRAUMA AND LOSS

For Abused Children and Abusive Parents

God who loves us as a faithful father,
God who loves us as a compassionate mother,
God who adopts us as beloved children,
hear my fervent prayer
for children who are abused and parents who abuse them.

I pray for abused children
in my class, in my community, in my church.
I can't always see them but I know they are there.
Their bodies are bruised and battered and worse.
Their spirits are sad and angry and worse.
Their minds are confused by adults
they cannot trust to take care of them.
Their hearts are broken by the very people
they love—and depend on—most.
I pray that the abuse will cease and they will be safe,
that their bodies and spirits and minds and hearts
will be healed and made whole,
that they will not repeat the cycle of abuse.

I pray for abusive parents.
I don't pretend to know
why they do it, or what stresses they face,
or what happened "to make them this way."
But I do know
that you love them and want them to know your love,
and by the power of your love, they can change.
I pray that they will learn a different way
to parent, to cope with stresses,
to deal with whatever factors made them this way.
I pray that the abuse will cease and their children will be safe,
that their children will not repeat the cycle of abuse.

I pray for myself
that I will find ways to help end child abuse,
that my love and prayers will contribute to healing and wholeness
for children who have been abused,
that my love and teaching will show children and their parents
a better way to live. Amen.

I Am a Mandated Reporter

God, I have to call
when I suspect a child is being abused.
I am a mandated reporter.
Give me eyes willing and able to see
physical signs of abuse.
Give me ears trained to hear between the lines
spoken signals of abuse.
Give me a heart full of compassion
open to discern when a child's spirit is breaking,
the abuse of a child's mind and heart.

God, when I call,
hear my prayer for the child I fear is being abused.
Keep her safe. Keep him secure.
Do not allow my call to become a trigger for more abuse.
For I confess . . . that is the fear
that sometimes keeps me from calling.

God, when I call,
hear my prayer for all those who will investigate.
Give them wisdom to discern
where there is abuse and where there is not.
Give them power to rescue and protect,
to end abuse where it is found,
to prevent further abuse.

God, make my call an instrument of your love,
saving and safeguarding one of your precious little ones,
a child you created,
a child you love,
a child you entrusted to our care.

Forgive us all
for ever allowing even one child to be abused.
Amen.

Dealing with Death

Word of God that offers wisdom and understanding,
I need your guidance.
Spirit of God that brings comfort and hope,
I need to feel you near.

This is one of those impossibly hard times
that teachers sometimes face,
dealing with the death of a child,
or the death of a parent
while children are still young,
deaths so untimely, so unfair, so unexplainable.

A six-year-old girl is dying of leukemia.
An eight-year-old boy died in a house fire.
The parents of two children, seven and ten,
were killed in an automobile accident.
A teenage girl committed suicide.
A teenage boy was hit by a drunk driver.

I need your help, God, to help my students,
to respond to their grief today
and for many days and weeks to come.
Attune my ears to hear their concerns and needs.
Guide my mouth to speak with compassion,
to give information that is accurate,
appropriate to their level of understanding
and to my role as their teacher.
Empower me to create within the classroom
a community that is caring and supportive
for each and all, according to their needs.

I need your help, God, to help my students' parents
and my colleagues, for they are mourning, too.

I need your help, God, for myself,
to heal the grief within my own heart.

Thank you, God, for the promises of faith.
You will hear my prayer and help me.
Your love gives us hope that overcomes sorrow,
life that is victorious even over death. Amen.

For Victims of Natural Disasters

God whose creative power formed the earth and sky and sea,
God whose loving power gives us birth, one and all,
God whose saving power conquers even death,
my heart aches, my spirit grieves, my soul prays
for children whose lives have been torn apart by natural disasters.

Hurricanes, earthquakes, howling winds, and forest fires.
Homes, schools, businesses, neighborhoods, jobs.
Treasured keepsakes, irreplaceable photographs.
Damaged, destroyed, devastated.
Lives and loved ones lost, disabled, and dead.

I am an adult. I cannot understand or even imagine it.
How much more difficult it must be for the children
who have experienced the unimaginable.
I weep with them. I weep for them.
My God, I believe you are weeping, too.

Hear my prayer for these children:
for reassurance when they are afraid,
for comfort when they are sad,
for hope when they are discouraged,
for friends when they are lonely,
for love surrounding and sustaining them
at all times and in all places.

Hear my prayer for the adults
who care for these children:
that they will be able
to ensure children's health and safety,
to reunite their families and friends,
to model resilience and renewal,
to rebuild schools and communities,
to provide love at all times and in all places.

Hear my prayer for rebirth,
for life that triumphs over death and destruction.
Hear my prayer for resurrection. Amen.

This prayer was written in September 2005 in the aftermath of Hurricane Katrina.

When There Is No Explanation

Tsunami. Hurricane. Earthquake.
More than words.
Images of destruction.
I can hardly bring myself
to listen to the radio
or read the paper or watch the news.
The stories and pictures
and video footage convey
more death and despair
than human hearts can bear,
more suffering and sorrow
than human minds can fathom.

If I am moved to tears,
if I cannot comprehend why such things happen,
how can I explain them to my students?

Almighty God,
there is much I do not know, much I cannot understand.
But this I do know.
You created the world, and called it good.
You love us so much that you sent Jesus to save us.
Your will for us is life,
lived with joy in unity with one another and with you.
I will not ever demean you with glib explanations
that such devastation is your will. It is not.

I believe that your tears mingle with my own.

Faithful God,
When disaster strikes, and I cannot understand,
give me just this,
the gift of your presence,
the comfort of your spirit.
When disaster strikes, and I cannot explain,
let me give to my students just this,
the gift of my presence,
the comfort of your spirit,
incarnate in me.
Amen.

7 ❋ Prayers for Parents and Families

A Child's First Teachers

It is so true.
For good or ill
parents are a child's first teachers.
Teaching her to trust the world.
Teaching him to walk confidently.
Teaching them to speak and listen.
Teaching her to ask questions.
Teaching him to play with others.
Teaching them to want to learn.
Teaching her honesty.
Teaching him compassion.
Teaching them what is good and right.
Or not.

God who creates each child
and entrusts every one

first to parents,
and then to others,
watch over with love
and guide with wisdom
children's parents,
their very first teachers.

God who places families
within a larger community,
watch over and guide all of us
to safeguard children
and support parents,
according to their need
so that children's first teachers
will be good teachers. Amen.

Beginning with Understanding

God whose Son is our Savior, Jesus the Christ,
God who invites us to become sons and daughters,
God who teaches us what it means to be family,
I pray for the families of my students.

I know I must pray for myself first.
Give me, O God, the ability to understand and accept
the families in which my students live
for they live in all different kinds of families.
Some live with their mothers and fathers and siblings.
Others live with stepparents and stepsiblings.
Some live with one parent and visit the other.
Others live with one parent and don't know the other.
Some live with grandparents.
Others live with older brothers or sisters, aunts or uncles.

Some live with adults who have adopted them.
Others live in foster care and homeless shelters.
Some share homes with one or two or many siblings.
Others are only children.
God who knows and understands all families,
today and every day, increase my understanding.

With understanding I can pray for my students' families,
for the parents and guardians with whom they live.
Give them, O God, the ability to love and care
for the children you have entrusted to them.
Some need more money
so that they can provide food, shelter, and medical care.
Others need more time
so that they can laugh and play and enjoy their children.
Some need to learn positive ways
to nurture their children's growth and development.
Others need to learn constructive ways
to solve problems and resolve conflicts.
Some need to "loosen the reins"
and let their children find their own way in the world.
Others need to "tighten the reins"
and show love for their children by setting limits.
God who knows and loves all families,
today and every day, increase their love and care.

With love I pray for all of us together,
for myself and my students' families, for our relationship.
Give us, O God, the ability to work together.
We need to understand and accept one another.
We need to love and care for each other.
We need time and trust and ways to communicate.
We need a shared vision and a spirit of cooperation.
God who knows and loves me,
God who knows and loves my students and their families,

today and every day, increase our ability to work together
so that my students who are their children
can learn and grow and become all that you intend.
Amen.

Working Together

God who gives the gift of children,
bless my work with their parents.

I'm a teacher.
I work every day with students
and often with their parents.
I'm a parent, too.
I know how good—and hard—that can be.

God who is patient with me
as a teacher and a parent,
help me to be a teacher who is patient
with the parents of my students.

Stop me when I start to judge them,
for that is your job alone.
Grant me the gift of empathy and compassion
so that I am able to understand
the challenges they face.
Guide me when I work with them
so that I am able to communicate in ways
they can hear and understand.
Empower us when we work together
so that I can be the best teacher possible
and they can be the best parents possible
for their unique and precious child.

God who is the Loving Parent of all of us,
I pray for my students and for their parents
and for our work together each day.
Amen.

⌾

Before the Parent-Teacher Conference

Gracious God,
Whose love gave birth to Jesus, the Son,
whose love for us is the wise and tender love
of a mother and father for their child,
hear my prayer as I get ready
to meet with the parents of my students.

Guide my preparation.
Help me to find the time
and spend the time needed
to think carefully about each student's
strengths and weaknesses,
accomplishments and challenges.

Guide my communication.
Give me the words, written and spoken,
that will allow me to say what needs to be said
honestly and compassionately.
Help me to identify specific suggestions
to share with parents
so that they can assist their sons and daughters.

Guide my heart.
Give me eyes to see, and ears to hear,
that I might accept and understand
each parent's point of view.

Give me love abundant,
that I might share your love
with my students and with their parents.
Amen.

Parent Volunteers

Thank you, God, for parents
who are actively involved
in their children's education.

For individual parent volunteers
who come into my class
each week or each month or
for special occasions.
Mothers who assist students
in learning centers and reading groups.
Fathers who attend field trips
and tutor students after school.
Their contribution of
time and energy and abilities
is an invaluable gift
to everyone's children.
Their selfless service to others
is an important model
for children and adults alike.

For groups of parent volunteers
who work together in organizations
like the PTA, or the PTO,
caring for children in schools and
advocating for children in society.
Sponsoring programs
to promote reading.

Donating funds for field trips
that were cut from the budget.
Building a playground
that is open to the community.
Lobbying for legislation
to protect children from abuse.
There are countless ways that
parents working together
can and do make a difference.

Thank you, God, for parents
whose active participation and support
improves the education of all children.
Amen.

The Hardest Job of All

Faithful father,
Loving mother,
Divine Parent,
it is the miracle of grace:
you have loved us
and adopted us as your children.
It is the miracle of life itself:
you have given us the gift of children
and called us to be parents in your image.

What an amazing gift.
What an awesome challenge.
I'm convinced.
Parenting is the hardest job there is.
To love our children as you love us
cannot be done without
your grace, your Son, your guiding Spirit.

Divine Parent,
I rejoice to be your child.
I sing and laugh and weep with thanksgiving
for the gift of children.
I pray for parents everywhere:
for my own parents,
for myself as a parent,
for the parents of my students,
for the parents and guardians
of all the children
in my home and classroom
and church and community.
I pray for parents and guardians
around the world.

Divine Parent,
by your love, teach us to love.
By your grace, may we show your amazing love
to all the children you have entrusted to our care.
Amen.

⁓

For My Own Family

Thank you, God, for family members
present and past, near and far,
who believe in the importance of teaching
and affirm that I have "what it takes,"
who support me in ways seen and unseen
and love me through the ups and downs of each year.
For my husband, who makes dinner when I am running late.
For my wife, who insists that I must stop work for the night.
For my daughter, who waits patiently while I answer a parent's call.
For my son, who beams with pride when he tells a friend

I'm a teacher.
For my brother, who understands because he's a teacher, too.
For my sister, who provides a respite because she isn't a teacher.
For my cousin, whose disabilities help me to be
more understanding.
For my parents, who taught me to follow Christ's call.
For my grandparents, who taught me to love learning.

Thank you, God, for the members of my family
whose support makes it possible for me to be a good teacher.
Help me to say and show my appreciation.
Help them to feel the depth of gratitude
that lies beyond expression.

Bless them, God, these family members
present and past, near and far.
Bless them with important work and the skills to do it well.
Bless them with supportive love that gets them through each day.

Thank you, God,
for the gift of your amazing love for me,
love made flesh in Jesus Christ.
I believe it is incarnate still
in the love that others show for me.
Bless me, God,
with the gift of your amazing love for others,
love made flesh in Jesus Christ.
May your love be incarnate still
in the love I show for them.
Amen.

8 ✿ Prayers for Educational Leadership

COLLEAGUES

We Are a Team

Triune God, Creator, Redeemer, Spirit,
Triune God, who is three-in-one,
Triune God, whose very essence is a team
with humility and with joy,
I give thanks
for the team of women and men
with whom I work.

When I consider
the responsibilities of teaching,
I am humbled.
I cannot do this job alone.
I need the support and encouragement,
the wisdom and guidance that
I receive from those around me.

When I consider
the responsibilities of teaching,
I rejoice
because I am not alone.
I am surrounded and sustained,
empowered to be a better teacher
by a team of amazing people.

Triune God,
I thank you for the team:
parent volunteers,
aides in the classroom,
teacher colleagues at every grade level,
diagnosticians and specialists,
service providers of every kind,
librarians, nurses, and
the school principal.

I pray for the team,
that we will work together
to teach the students
whom you have entrusted to us.
Amen.

Remembering Those Usually Forgotten

God of all people,
I pray every day for my students.
I pray every day for myself.

Today I want to pray for people I usually forget to pray for:
bus drivers and crossing guards,
teacher aides and parent volunteers,
cafeteria cooks and lunchroom monitors,
custodians and security guards.

All of these people—and more—
are part of the learning community in this school.
All of them touch the lives
of the students who come here to learn and grow.
All of them have the opportunity and the responsibility
to make this a place of learning and success for all students.

God of the unseen and oft forgotten,
hear my prayer for those whom I too often overlook.
Give these school workers what they need
to fulfill their responsibilities:
health and happiness at home so that
they can come to work unburdened;
abilities and experiences that have prepared them
to do their jobs well;
values and behaviors that make them
good role models for students;
hearts and minds that are open
to care for young and old in this community.

God of the unseen and oft forgotten,
forgive me for overlooking anyone in this school.
Give me eyes to see others,
a heart open to care for them,
a collegial spirit ready to work with them
to make this a place of learning and success for all people.
Give me faith to pray for them every day.
Amen.

The Teachers' Lounge

Jesus commanded us to pray:
Lead us not into temptation,
but deliver us from evil.

How tempting it is
to gather in the teachers' lounge
to gossip.
How easily the words flow
complaining about students and parents
who push us to the limits of our abilities
and our patience.
How easily the words flow
spilling out for our colleagues
tales from our own experiences of students
that will bias the expectations of others.
How easily the words flow
recounting information shared in confidence
betraying those who have trusted us.
O God, I pray: deliver us from this evil.

Jesus commanded us to love:
Love the Lord your God with all your being.
Love your neighbor as yourself.

How important it is
to gather in the teachers' lounge
to nurture relationships with one another,
to create a community of colleagues.
How special are the moments when we are able
to celebrate together
individual joys and shared successes,
to weep together over
personal sorrows and shared disappointments,
to learn from one another
strategies for teaching and motivating our students.
O God, I pray: teach us to love.

Teach us to love you, and to show our love for you
by loving our neighbors in classrooms and offices,
and in the teachers' lounge. Amen.

Colleagues Alike and Different

Thank you, God, for my colleagues at school.

Thank you for colleagues
who share my Christian faith
with whom I can study and pray
and discuss how to live faithfully at school
as models of the love and grace
you have revealed to us in Christ Jesus.

Thank you also for colleagues
who do not share my faith,
for those of every tradition—
Jews, Muslims, Hindus, and more—
and for those who have no religion.
Thank you for women and men
who are different from me,
who remind me of the diversity of humanity,
who challenge me to love with your love
not only people who are like me, but all people,
because you created and love them.
Thank you for opportunities
to learn from the exchange of different ideas, and
to celebrate the commonalities
that we discover among the differences.

Thank you, God, for colleagues alike and different.
Thank you that we share a commitment
to providing an excellent education
for all the children of our community.

Thank you, God, for colleagues alike and different.
By your grace and the power of your love,
may we work together to create a community of learning
in which all are respected and appreciated,
in which all learn and grow toward the fullness of life
that you intend and that you give. Amen.

The Character of Coaches

God who fashioned our marvelous bodies,
God who gives each of us unique abilities,
I never cease to be amazed by the talents
shown by some of the students at school.
Fred is an incredible gymnast.
Mark is a star basketball player.
Alexa could get a hockey scholarship.
The volleyball team is going to make it
to the state championship this year.

God in Christ, who is my friend and my life coach,
I thank you for these students, and I pray for their coaches.

I pray for the women and men
who coach individual athletes and sports teams,
whose every interaction with girls and boys
is an opportunity to nurture their physical abilities,
and an occasion to promote positive character.
I pray that these women and men
will be models of integrity and character:
showing respect for students' bodies,
their care and limits as well as their potential;
demonstrating that hard work and fair play
are more important than winning;
teaching them to be good sports
who have fun even when they lose;
encouraging them to become a team of athletes
who support and encourage each other.

God in Christ, who came to save us from our sin,
I confess that I know these women and men
sometimes lose perspective or self-control or character.
And so I pray also for the rest of us,
principals and teachers, umpires and parents, that

we will have the courage to speak up
and hold coaches accountable for their character.

I pray for coaches, that by their integrity and character,
they will nurture the integrity and character
as well as the bodies of student athletes. Amen.

The Teachers' Union

God who gives voice to the voiceless,
who seeks justice and righteousness in all things:

I believe that you want teachers
to have a voice in making decisions that affect
students and their learning, and
teachers and their working conditions.
I believe that you want teachers
to use their voice to secure what is just:
fair wages, adequate benefits, time to plan,
and the resources to teach all children well.

I believe that sometimes
it is important and necessary for teachers
to come together in a professional union
that can be the voice speaking for them.
I give thanks for the times that
unions have worked collaboratively
with school and district leadership
to support student learning and
to meet teachers' needs.
I regard with frustration times that
unions have failed to work cooperatively.
I regard with shame times that
unions have sought power over progress,

sacrificing students and their learning
to obtain for teachers
more than what is just and necessary.

Whether I choose to be a union member, or
I am a union member because I have no choice, or
I choose not to be a union member,
this is my prayer:
Give me a voice, O God, that speaks for justice.
Make me an advocate of justice for teachers,
not for the sake of teachers or teachers' unions,
but for the sake of the students we teach.
Make me an advocate of justice for students,
that they will all have excellent teachers and
every opportunity to learn. Amen.

SCHOOL AND DISTRICT LEADERS

The Power of a Principal

Leader of the school building.
Usually the person with the most say
about who is hired and who gets tenure.
Always the person whose spirit
determines the educational environment.
Organized or chaotic.
Collegial or dictatorial.
Inspiring teachers or asking little of them.
Challenging students or expecting little.
Holding everyone to high standards or
accepting mediocrity and even failure.
The principal has tremendous power
to shape the experiences

of teachers and students and parents,
to affect, for better or worse,
students' learning and achievement.

I pray for my principal.
Thank you that she is willing to serve this way.
I know it is not an easy job.
I pray for my principal.
Bless him with understanding and skills,
the gift of leadership.
I know it is not an easy job.

God of power and wisdom and love,
grant that my principal will use the power of this office
to nurture an effective educational environment
in which teachers and students delight to work together
to meet the challenge of reaching the highest standards
of teaching and learning and living with love.

God who leads my life,
I pray for the leader of my school building. Amen.

The Superintendent

Who would want her position?
Who would want to do what he has to do?
I thank you, God, that someone wants this job!

I thank you, God, for the women and men
who are willing to become superintendents,
leaders of school districts, large and small.
I thank you for each one who is willing
to use talents and experiences you have provided,
to engage in the education and training required,

to accept responsibility for oversight of so many
people and programs, facilities and monies.
I thank you for each one who is willing
to do this important work, even when it means
navigating a seemingly endless stream of
conflicts to be resolved and criticism to be endured.
It is a big—and so often thankless—job.
I thank you, God. Remind me
to thank the person who is my superintendent.

I pray, God, for the men and women
who are the superintendents of districts near and far.
I pray that each superintendent will do the job well:
that each will have "what it takes"
in education, experience, and character
to be an effective leader and role model
for the people working together to serve students.
I pray that each superintendent will be empowered
by the support and collaboration of others:
competent faculty and staff in the schools,
involved parents of students at every grade level,
a community that values and votes for education,
a Board of Education that governs wisely.
I pray that each superintendent will be respected:
afforded time for leisure as well as work,
valued in relationships as a human being,
honored for success as an educational leader.
Remind me, God, to pray each day
for the person who is my superintendent. Amen.

The Board of Education

Elected or appointed, few or many,
the Board of Education exercises great authority,
and has a tremendous impact on schools,
administrators, teachers, parents, and,
most significant of all, the students they serve.

God, who bids me pray for all people,
hear my prayer for the Board of Education.
I pray for the board as a team of leaders.
I pray that board members will be a team.
I pray that they will be leaders.

God, whose loving spirit
enables people to work together,
guide the work of this team.
Grant them the ability, one and all,
to listen to each other and the community,
to speak thoughtfully and clearly,
to argue fairly and respectfully,
to make decisions using processes
that they all can support—whatever the outcome.

God, whose wisdom
enables people to be leaders,
guide the work of these officials.
Bestow upon them, one and all,
the qualities of leadership:
responsibility, character, and wisdom.
Empower them to fulfill their duties competently.
Inspire them to demonstrate integrity at all times.
Direct them to make sound choices,
decisions that will make it possible for schools
to provide an excellent education for all students.

I also pray for the board as a group of people:
for their personal health and energy,

their satisfaction at work and home.
I thank you, God, for Board of Education members,
and pray that they will experience
the respect and appreciation of others. Amen.

The Board–Superintendent Relationship

The Board of Education and
the Superintendent of Schools
have to work together.
They must. That's all there is to it.
They have to know their respective roles,
and they have to do their respective jobs,
capably and collaboratively.
The education of students depends on it
in our district and every district.

God who works through human activity
to accomplish divine purposes,
grant that the relationship
between our board and superintendent
might be a true partnership
characterized by trust and mutual respect,
energized by optimism and hope,
guided by a deep commitment to children
and the education children need,
the excellent education children deserve
from this district and community.

God, work through these human leaders,
that, empowered to be effective partners,
they might accomplish your purposes
for the children they serve. Amen.

School Budgets

Public schools funded by public monies.
Resources allocated and policies determined
by multiple levels of public officials.

Bountiful God, you give to us all of life's resources.
Just God, it is your holy will that we use them wisely.
Accept this prayer of thanksgiving and petition
for public schools and public school budgets.

I believe in public schools.
I believe it is the public's responsibility to educate
all of the children you have placed in our midst.
Thank you, God,
for the resources provided by the community,
time and energy, goodwill, and, yes, money.
Thank you, God,
for the people whose decisions govern the schools,
boards of education, city councils, state legislatures.

I pray for public schools.
I pray that they will be well-funded and fairly governed.
God, grant that all citizens of every community
will have wise minds and generous hearts,
willing to support the funding of school budgets.
God, grant that public officials at every level
will have wise minds and generous hearts,
able to make sound and equitable decisions
about how to allocate school budget resources.

God who loves each of us individually,
God who loves us all without exception,
whether we are mothers and fathers
or adults without children,
whether we send our children to public schools,

choose schools sponsored by faith communities,
or choose other private schools,
guide us—empower us—to support public schools,
to promote the education and well-being of all children,
not just a few, not just our own. Amen.

9 ✻ Prayers for People and Communities of Faith

Teaching Is My Ministry

I live in two worlds.

I teach children.
Every day I see
how much they have to give to the community, and
how much they need from the community.

I go to church.
Every Sunday I am reminded
of the church's responsibility to serve the community,
of the call to minister to people in need in Christ's name.

God, who is One,
bring my worlds together,
unite my work and faith.

Help me to understand that
it is you who have given me gifts to teach,

it is you who have set me among children in need.
Help me to affirm in mind and heart that
being a teacher is ministering to children in Christ's name.

Merciful God, I dare to ask one more thing.
When I cannot serve on a church committee
or say yes to another request
because of the time I give to teaching,
please
help my church to understand and affirm that
being a teacher is ministering to children in Christ's name.
Amen.

For My Church Community

God, whose very being is community,
Blessed Trinity, Three Persons in One,
God, who created us to live in community,
many members, one body in Christ:
Thank you for my church community.

Thank you, God, for the seed of faith
that you planted in my heart.

Thank you, God, for the church community
that nurtures my always growing faith,
people who teach and care for me,
people who worship and serve with me,
people whose loving witness to Christ
embodies your love for me.
Guide me, O God, that I, too,
might nurture the faith of others
and embody your love for them.

Thank you, God, for the divine Word
spoken to me through the church community,
the Word of amazing grace that saves me,
the Word of commission that calls me to serve others,
the Word of hope that promises you are with me.
Guide me, O God, that I
might live with grace, serving others,
trusting in your presence always.

Thank you, God,
for the opportunity and the challenge
to live my faith and serve you every day,
at home and at work in my classroom.
Thank you for the support I receive
from my church community.
Thank you for the guidance I find
hearing your Word and feeling your presence.
Today and every day. Amen.

Accepting Responsibility for All Children

Creator whose love gives birth to children,
Redeemer who came to earth as a child,
Spirit of God speaking through children everywhere:

Economists tell us children are a "public good."
We know that they are so much more.
As Jesus did so long ago,
you have set children in the midst of us.
You love them.
You have entrusted them to our care.

Thank you for the gift of children in our community.
Thank you for the children who squirm in the pew next to me.

Thank you for the children who live in the house next door.
Thank you for the children on bicycles and school buses.
Thank you for the children selling lemonade on the corner
and playing baseball in the field.

Forgive us for neglecting the children in our community.
Forgive us for thinking they are someone else's problem.
Forgive us for believing that parents can raise them without help.
Forgive us for shortchanging the schools that educate them.
Forgive us for allowing one child to be hungry or homeless or
    abused.

Teach us all to accept responsibility for all of the children
in our midst.
Empower us to be instruments of your loving care.
Empower parents to care for their children
and their children's friends and their neighbors' children.
Empower schools to care for children
by helping students to grow in knowledge, and also in virtue.
Empower churches and temples and mosques to care for children
by working together to create a safe and supportive community.
Empower community organizations, business leaders, and
    government officials
to care for children through people and programs that
protect and nurture them.

Children are a gift that you have entrusted to our care.
Teach us all to accept responsibility for all of the children
in our midst.
Empower me to be an instrument of your love for children.
Amen.

10 ❋ Prayers for the School Year

Day One

Faithful God,
who was, and is, and shall be,
Alpha and Omega,
beginning and ending.

This is the beginning of a new year.

Today I will welcome a new class of students.
Today I will start to connect names and faces.
Today I will begin to learn about their diverse
interests and abilities and personalities.
Today I will tell them something about myself
and what we will do together this year.

Let me begin this year with prayer.

I pray for my students,
for their safety and health

in body, mind, and spirit.
I pray that they will learn—and
that they will love learning.

I pray for myself
that I will come to know each of them,
that I will show love for every one,
that I will teach them all effectively,
honoring their unique interests and abilities and personalities.

I pray for the year ahead,
that we will grow together in knowledge and love
to your everlasting glory.

Let me begin this year, this day, every day with prayer.
Amen.

Butterflies — Mine and Theirs

A new school year. Beginning again.
Fresh faces. A fresh start.
No matter how many times I go through it,
there will always be something special
about this time of year.

Butterflies in my stomach.
I am awed by the responsibilities.
Anxious anticipation.
I am excited by the possibilities.

Butterflies in their stomachs.
Students apprehensive about challenges ahead.
Anxious anticipation.
Students still eager to learn.

Prayers of thanksgiving
for each and every student,
for the privilege of teaching,
for the butterflies
that energize my preparation,
that drive me to reflect and improve,
that keep me humble.

Prayers for guidance
for myself and my colleagues,
that we might teach well,
for myself and my students,
that we might learn well.

God who watches over me,
hear my prayers
spoken and silent
as I begin a new school year.
Amen.

An Open Mind and Heart

God of all knowledge,
you know me better than I know myself.
God of endless mercy,
you accept me just as I am.
God of amazing grace,
you love me into becoming more than I am.

God, be with me as I start a new school year.
Give me an open mind and heart.

Save me from temptation,
that I may not let

my knowledge of students
be prejudiced by the words or experiences of others,
my acceptance of students
be contingent on their behaving the way I want them to, or
my love for students
be limited by the ways they are different from me.

Fill me with your Spirit,
that I may
come to know my students well,
accept them just as they are, and
love them into becoming all that you intend.

God, be with me as I start a new school year.
Give me an open mind and heart,
that I may be an instrument of your loving grace.
Amen.

Jewish Holy Days

God of the Covenant,
this is the holiest time of year
for my Jewish brothers and sisters.
This is the time when they repent
and celebrate the promise of a new year.
So may it also be for me
a time of repentance and renewal.

Forgive my arrogance.
Forgive any thought or deed
that suggests my faith makes me superior to others.

Forgive my prejudice.
Forgive me for accepting as truth
the biases and stereotypes that surround me.

Forgive my forgetfulness.
Forgive me for failing to see how my own faith
is rooted and grounded in the history of Israel,
in your covenant with the Jewish people.

Give me a renewed mind and heart.
Increase my understanding of Judaism, past and present.
Increase my compassion for Jewish people, near and far.

I pray for my Jewish students as they observe
the holy days of Rosh Hashanah and Yom Kippur.
Help me to understand and love each of them.
Help me to create a classroom community
in which they all feel respected and valued every day.

God of the Covenant,
You are their God. You are my God. You are One.
Amen.

On Christopher Columbus and Political Correctness

God who is the Author of history,
why is it that they keep rewriting history?
How can they say (whoever they are)
"Christopher Columbus did not discover the New World"?

I question and complain because change is hard and because
the voices calling for change sometimes seem so extreme.
I do not want to change to be politically correct.
Yet I also understand that change is necessary, and sometimes
voices calling for change are, like prophets of old, speaking for you.
I do want to change to be more faithful to your holy will.

God, I am trying to sort this out.
I know beyond all doubt your love is the most amazing,
most powerful gift ever given, not earned, not deserved,
not reserved for some, but a gift for all:
people of every race and language, every time and place.
I also know beyond all defenses that in human history
we have not lived with such equal love for all.
Some people have been privileged:
their stories told, their accomplishments revered,
their wealth increased, at the expense of others.
Other people have been oppressed:
their voices silenced, their achievements unknown,
their poverty ignored, as they waited on others.

Ever so slowly, God, I am beginning to understand.
We do not need to rewrite history, but to re-learn it,
from the perspective of those whose stories were not told.
It is true that Christopher Columbus sailed west
and landed among the Caribbean islands.
It is also true that the story of Europeans
who settled among native populations is decidedly mixed:
a tale of discovery and destruction, cooperation and conflict.
It is worth knowing the whole story.

Author of all history and Creator of all people,
help me to learn and teach the whole history of your people,
not to be politically correct, but to live with your love for all.
Because your unchanging love changes everything.
Amen.

What to Do About Halloween?

The days are shorter.
The leaves are falling.
The pumpkins are ripe.
There are bags of candy on sale everywhere.
O God, it's Halloween again.
I'll be honest.
I really don't know what to make
of this particular autumn holiday.

I give thanks for healthy fun:
the simple pleasure
of dressing up in a costume,
the shared joy
of parties and games
and a few sweet treats.

I confess my anxiety about all that is not healthy:
overindulgences—
too much money spent,
too much hype, and too much candy;
children and adults alike
who are frightened by
vandalism, the threat of violence, and
so-called practical jokes that are not funny;
a morbid fascination with destructive powers,
as if evil were a trivial matter.

God who is faithful in all seasons,
hear my prayer during this Halloween season.
Show me how to use my mixed feelings
to encourage and promote all that is good,
to discourage and limit that which is not.
Help me to model for my students—whatever their ages—
life-giving ways to celebrate this and every holiday.

God who loves every child, costumed and not,
hear my prayer for my students at Halloween,
Watch over each one. Keep them all safe.
In the name of the One who came as a child,
Jesus the Christ.
Amen.

Election Day: Rights and Responsibilities

God of all nations,
I am thankful that I am an American citizen.
I give thanks for the rights and
accept the responsibilities that I have.
At this election time, especially,
I give thanks for my right to vote, and
accept the responsibility to be an informed voter.
Give me wisdom and understanding
so that I will exercise my right responsibly.

God of all nations,
As a teacher in this nation, it is my job
to help students understand their rights and responsibilities
and, even more, to challenge and inspire them
to appreciate their rights and accept their responsibilities.
Give me wisdom and enthusiasm
so that I will do my job effectively.
Amen.

Thanks-giving

Thank you, God, for this day set aside
to give you thanks.
There is so much that I am thankful for.

I am thankful for my life,
for my heart and mind and body.
I am thankful for the lives
of those who love and care for me—
family and friends, near and far.

I am thankful for my job as a teacher
for the privilege and the challenge
of helping students to learn and grow.
I am thankful for students present and past
who have challenged me to learn and grow.

I am thankful for my faith,
for the power of your abundant love,
for the gift of your amazing grace,
for the guidance of your Holy Spirit, and
for the church community
in which my faith is nurtured and grows.

I am thankful for the time
to gather with family and friends
to share good food and relaxed conversation,
to rest from work and catch up on sleep!

Thank you, God, for Thanksgiving!
As I enjoy this special day of celebration,
remind me to give thanks every day.
There is so much to be thankful for.
Amen.

Signs of Christmas

Oh, God. It's December.
The Christmas chaos has begun.
Garland on poles, lights on houses,
lines at the store, catalogs at home,
adults in a hurry, children in a frenzy,
Santa's making his list,
signs of Christmas are everywhere.
Or are they?

O, my God. It's Advent.
A time of anticipation. Waiting.
Knowing you will come. Wondering.
How will you come?
What will be the signs of your presence?
What are the signs of Christmas?

Jesus, born of Mary, laying in a manger,
God Incarnate, the Word made flesh.
They knew you would come, but not how.
That was a surprise, a miracle,
a sign that only a few could see.

O, my God. It's Advent.
In this holy season of waiting,
I am watching for signs of your coming.
Help me not to confuse
the glow of bright lights or
the bustle of holiday activity with
the real signs of your Christmas gift.
Open my eyes to see you in surprising places:
the faces of my students,
the community of my classroom,
my friendship with colleagues,

our partnership with parents.
Open my heart to experience anew the miracle:
you are born and live among us, fully human, fully God.

I know that you have come, and you will come again.
I do not know how. That is always a surprise. A miracle.
Give me the eyes of faith, O God, that I may see.
Amen.

Lord, Slow Me Down

The month of December
preparing for Christmas
such a busy time.

In addition to the usual demands of teaching
I'm trying to shop and wrap and bake,
write cards and send packages, and
attend special events at school and church.
In addition to the usual classroom commotion,
the kids at school are acting crazy,
full of sugar and frantic with anticipation.

Lord, slow me down.
Keep me from
trying to do too much.
Remind me not
to buy too much,
to bake too much,
to go too much,
to worry too much.
I can't do it all.
Trying to do it all
misses the point anyway.

Lord, slow me down.
Keep me from adding
to my students' frenzy.
Help me to bring calm
to my classroom.

Lord, slow me down.
Keep me from missing the point.
Help me to calm my heart
so that I am prepared for Christmas.
Help me to open my heart
to receive again your gift of amazing love
made flesh in Jesus the Christ.
Amen.

The Gift of a Child

A baby crying.
Asleep in a hay box.
Nursing at Mary's breast.
Cradled in Joseph's arms.
Fully human.
Angels in the heavens.
A star in the east.
Attended by shepherds and sages.
Long-awaited Son of God.
Fully divine.

Wondrous love revealed
in the gift of a child.

God-with-us in Jesus Christ,
as we prepare
to celebrate his birth, and

receive anew
this gift of love incarnate,
help us to see your love revealed
in the gift of every child.

God-with-us in Jesus Christ,
beside me in the classroom,
help me to receive each student
as a gift from you.
Help me to see your love revealed
in each boy and girl.
Help me to love with your love
every student in my class.

To you, O God, be
all praise and honor and thanksgiving
for your wondrous love
revealed in the gift of a child.
Amen.

December Dilemmas

Hanukkah. Christmas. Sometimes Ramadan. Kwanzaa.
December is a month of diverse holidays and traditions.

I am a teacher in a public school.
I cannot do anything
that imposes observance of one faith
upon students of other faiths.
I am a Christian teacher
in a school and community where
the majority celebrates Christmas.
I do not want to impose our faith.
What to do in December is a dilemma.

God whose coming in Christ I will soon celebrate,
guard my words and actions throughout this month
so that in all things I demonstrate respect
for all people and for our varied faith traditions.

When the curriculum calls for me
to teach my students about religious holidays,
mine and theirs and those of others not in the class,
may my lessons be accurate and informative,
neither devotional nor dismissive, but truly educational.

When students call upon me to have a Christmas party,
help me to find the words to explain the difference
between learning about a holiday and celebrating it.
Help me to plan December activities that are special and fun
without asking students to celebrate a holiday not their own.

When the school schedule calls for a concert,
let me be a leader working with other teachers
to ensure that the music performed represents
a diversity of religious and secular traditions.

God whose coming in Christ I will soon celebrate,
guide me through the dilemmas of these December days
so that my genuine respect and understanding of others
might be a living channel of your love for all people.
Love incarnate.
Amen.

When Winter Gets Me Down

Naked branches
shadows against a gray sky.
Snowflakes swirling
whipped by a howling wind.
Days that seem
so short, so dark.
In the dead of winter
it is sometimes easy
to be discouraged,
disheartened, depressed.
In the dead of winter
it is sometimes hard
to be cheerful,
lighthearted, hopeful.
In the dead of winter
it is sometimes difficult
to get up and go to school
and model
the love of life and learning.

God of all seasons,
when winter gets me down,
lift me up.
God of all days,
when darkness overwhelms me,
shine your light upon me.
God of all life,
when depression threatens,
fill me with your hope.
God of my life,
when it is hard for me to get up and go to school,
help me.

Restore my energy and enthusiasm
so that I can model the love of life and learning.
Renew my faith in your promises.
Spring follows winter.
Light overcomes darkness.
Hope defeats despair.
In Jesus Christ life conquers death.
Amen.

Black History Month

Praise God! You are the Liberator.
Working through unlikely leaders and
speaking through messengers of old,
you led the Hebrew people out of slavery
into the promised land.
Working through the Civil War
and the civil rights movement,
speaking through modern prophets
and the leaders of our time,
you freed the slaves in our nation
and created for them a more just land.
But it is not yet the promised land.

During this month of February
I thank you, God, for every opportunity
to learn and teach my students about the rich history
of our African-American brothers and sisters,
to confront the harm they have endured,
and celebrate their myriad accomplishments.
But that is not enough.

Lead me, God, to use this time
to deepen students' respect and appreciation,

but also to help them see the continuing need
and commit to joining the ongoing struggle
to free African Americans from racism,
to ensure true equality of opportunity,
to establish the liberty and justice for all
that we claim so proudly but often fail to deliver.

Lead me, God, to make this time
just one part of my own year-long, lifelong effort
to be your messenger, a leader in this time,
proclaiming release to the captives,
freedom to all who are oppressed.
In the name of Christ, whose liberty
I accept as the gift of your amazing grace.
Amen.

Valentine's Day

Excited elementary students
stuffing handmade mailboxes
with tiny paper valentines.
A shy middle school student
leaving an anonymous note
for a special friend to find.
Enchanted high school students
offering their first romantic gift,
a sentimental card, a red rose.
Valentine's Day is celebrated at school
with all the pride and pleasure that come
from giving and receiving
signs of love and friendship.
Valentine's Day at school is also marked
by all the pain and loneliness that result
when one is left out of the exchange.

No matter the age,
girls and boys long
to be among those who are remembered
when valentines are distributed,
to be included in some way
in the relationships celebrated this day.
No matter the age,
no girl or boy wants to be the one left out.

Magnificent God,
whose heart of love embraces each of us,
whose depth of love surpasses our understanding,
to the extent that I have any authority,
let me use it to ensure that all are included.
To the degree that students' actions are beyond my control
hear the prayers of my heart for those who are left out.
May my words and deeds be sensitive and caring,
appropriate expressions of my Christian love for them,
a vehicle by which they experience the gift of your love.
For it is your love that saves us, today and every day.
Amen.

A Day Off!

Thank you, God, for days off!
A Monday holiday.
No classes on Friday.
The unexpected gift of a snow day
in the middle of the week.

Thank you, God,
that here and there
scattered throughout the school year
there are days in the week

usually planned, sometimes a surprise
when I don't have to go to school.

No matter how much I love my work,
no matter how deep is my commitment to students,
I need an occasional break, and they do, too.

I need personal time,
a long weekend when I can travel to visit family,
a weekday available for doctors' appointments,
an unanticipated but joyfully received
opportunity to catch up on things I've put off,
like calling a special friend, reading a good book,
even cleaning the house or paying the bills.

Thank you, God, for the gift of time.
Time at work and time at home.
Teaching time and personal time.

Thank you, God, that today is a day off!
Amen.

The Miracle of Easter

Hallelujah! Christ the Lord is risen!
This is the miracle we celebrate at Easter.
The fullness of this miracle is more
than we can understand or put into words,
but I rejoice because this I know.

God whose love raised Christ from the dead,
your love is the greatest power in all the universe.
Your love conquers sin and evil.
Your love is the promise of new life even in death.
Your love cannot be overcome or taken from us.

God whose love is the power of the resurrection,
help me to live with resurrection faith.

When I am moved to anger by the power of sin:
children abandoned and abused,
teenage victims and perpetrators of violence,
school district funds embezzled by corrupt officials,
help me to trust that the power of your love is greater still.
Let your love work through me to defeat human sin.

When I am moved to tears by the tragedies of life:
children who lose parents in a car accident,
a teenager dying of cancer,
families without homes following a hurricane,
help me to believe the promise that new life is possible still.
Let your love work through me to bring new life into being.

When I am moved to despair by whatever cause:
conflict within my own family,
a sense of inadequacy as a teacher,
guilt that I am not wholly faithful,
help me to be renewed by your ever-present love in my life.
Let your love work though me to share the good news with others:
There is nothing in all of life that can separate us from your love,
revealed in the Son who lived and died and was raised from the dead.

Christ the Lord is risen! Hallelujah!
Amen.

High Stakes, High Anxiety

In the days before yet another end-of-the-year
high-stakes assessment of state learning standards,
a fourth grader asked,
"Does fourth grade count for the rest of your life?"

O, my God, what have we come to?
How and why have we designed a system
that elicits such anguish from a nine-year-old child?

I believe in standards.
I want children to learn all that they can.
I want them to be fully prepared to live
as responsible, successful citizens
in an ever-changing multicultural world.
I believe in assessment.
I know that it is important to measure students' learning.
I know that regular assessment encourages students
to engage in the thinking processes that facilitate learning.
I believe in accountability.
I accept the challenge to be an effective teacher.
I accept responsibility for my students' learning.

But there must be a better way.
There must be a way to teach and measure learning
that will sustain children's natural curiosity,
that will encourage their pursuit of understanding,
that will motivate them to work toward excellence.
There must be a way to teach and measure learning
without so many hurtful consequences.

God who teaches us how to live with faith,
God who measures our faithfulness
and forgives us when we fall short,
forgive us now

for the needless anxiety and fear and pain
that students and parents experience
because of the way we teach and measure learning.
Show us now the better way.
God, show us how to teach our students
the lessons that really do count for the rest of their lives.
Amen.

Test Fatigue

Saving God whose burden is light,
Caring God who has promised rest to the weary,
I confess
I am tired.
My students are tired.
I'm not sure that I—or they—can take one more test.
It's that time of year
when it seems as if all my students do is take tests.
Ease their burden.
Give us rest.

I have taught them as well as I know how.
They have prepared as much as they can.
We all know
the necessity and the inadequacy
of summative assessments.
We need some measure of what they have learned
but there is no way to measure all they have learned.
How much less can we measure
the life lessons that are most important to learn.

Ever-present God
who walks beside us each day,
give us stamina to get through these days.

Help me to model patience and perseverance.
Help my students to do their best,
to demonstrate as fully as possible what they have learned,
yes, for others,
but more importantly, for themselves.
Bring us to that day when we can celebrate together:
The tests are over!
And I can say to them:
Wow! Look how much you've learned!
Amen.

End-of-the-Year Celebrations

Yes, God! Hallelujah!
The end of the school year.
It's finally here. Hooray!
We've all worked hard.
It's time to celebrate.

Parties in each class.
A field trip for the sixth graders.
Field days for the whole school.
A picnic for the yearbook staff.
Pizza and wings on the last day.
A reception to honor the senior class.
So many ways to celebrate.

God who gives us learning and growth,
God whose spirit sustains us in hard times,
God who rejoices with us in good times,
accept this song of praise and thanksgiving
for all the blessings of the school year ending.
Praise for all that we have learned!
Praise for all the ways we have worked together!

Praise for perseverance that got us through!
Praise for growth in mind and body and spirit!
Praise for every opportunity to celebrate life!
God who has been our help in all times past,
God who is our hope for all future times,
accept our song of praise and thanksgiving
as together we celebrate the end of the school year.
Hallelujah. Hooray!
Amen.

Prayers for the Seasons of Teaching

11 ❀

My First Teaching Job!

God of all time, past and present:
I can't believe it. The long-awaited time is here!
I'm a certified teacher. I have my first job.

Thank you for everything
that has led me to this moment:
from my earliest school experiences as a child
to my most recent, an adult student just last semester;
from my best teachers, whom I seek to emulate
to my worst, those who taught me what not to do;
from babysitting for my neighbors
to teaching Sunday school;
from counseling children in outdoor camps
to tutoring students in urban classrooms;
from reading textbooks and taking tests about tests
to writing standards-based lesson plans;

from countless hours observing others
to nervous hours being observed as a student teacher.

God of the past,
I know that you have been beside me, leading me,
working through the experiences of my life
to prepare me to become an effective teacher.

God of the present,
I know that you are here beside me, leading me still.
Help me to feel your presence.
Calm the anxiety bursting my heart,
a bubbling blend of excitement and fear.
Guide the decisions I must make,
curriculum, instruction, assessments, and more.
Imbue with your spirit the relationships I will develop
with students, parents, and colleagues.

God-beside-me, past and present,
Help me to feel your presence as I begin my first teaching job.
Lead me. Empower me.
Show me the way and give me the power
to be an effective . . . no, more—an excellent—teacher.
In your name and for your glory.
Amen.

After the First Few Months

My first year of teaching.
A few months done.
Many more to go.
I'm exhilarated.
I love my job.
I'm exhausted.

I knew it would be a lot of work
but I didn't know how much.
I think it will get easier
but I'm not sure when.

Thank you, God,
for the first tastes of the rewards of teaching,
wide grins and high fives,
light bulbs going on,
the whispered request from a trusting student,
"Can we talk?"
Thank you, God,
for treasured moments
that make all the work worthwhile.

Help me, God,
to face the special challenges of the first year,
learning the culture of the school,
teaching the curriculum for the first time,
getting to know colleagues and community expectations.
Help me, God,
to find the time and energy
to do all the work that must be done
and to do it well.

Exhilarated and exhausted.
I give myself to you, O God, just as I am.
Bless this, my first year of teaching.
Amen.

I'm Going to Be Observed

The principal. Human resource manager.
Team leader. Superintendent.
Whoever it is . . . will be coming soon
to observe my teaching and evaluate me.
I'm a good teacher. But I still get anxious.
I want to do my best.

God of the past,
thank you for being my help and guide,
leading me to teach in this time and place.

God of the present,
I ask that you will be with me now
to help and guide me
as I prepare for this evaluation.
Lead me to use my time wisely
to do what I know how to do well,
to develop clear objectives
and sound lesson plans
that use varied strategies
to engage diverse learners.

God of the (very near) future,
I pray that you will be with me on that day
to help and guide me
while I'm being observed.
Calm my fears so that I will be able
to demonstrate strong teaching skills
that effectively assist students
in meeting the lesson objectives.
When it's over, lead me to be reflective,
willing to ask myself, "What could I do better?"
and open to hear others' feedback, too.

God of all time, with your help and guidance,
I will do my best teaching,
and this observation will be an opportunity
to make my teaching even better.
That is the point, right?! Amen!

∞

I Have a Student Teacher

It seems like not that long ago
I was a student teacher.
Now I'm an experienced teacher
who has accepted responsibility
for a student teacher in my classroom.

I'm excited.
I enjoy being a mentor,
sharing what I have learned over the years.
I know I will also learn in the process of
explaining to him why I do what I do, and
seeing the different strategies that she uses.

I'm anxious, too.
I don't know yet how well we'll get along,
how effective she will be, or
how much coaching he will need.
Having assistance will free up some time,
but providing assistance will take time.

God-in-Christ, my ever-present mentor,
I lift to you my enthusiasm and concern.
I pray for myself and my student teacher.
Make me an effective supervisor:
modeling best practices myself,
watching him frequently and fairly,

giving her honest and constructive feedback,
providing adequate opportunities
for my student teacher to teach,
to learn from failures as well as successes,
and then to teach again.
Give to the person who is my student teacher
a willingness to plan ahead and work hard,
a mind open to new ideas and varied approaches,
a heart full of compassion for students,
the ability to become an effective teacher.
Bless our relationship with your life-giving Spirit
that our time together might be
a time of learning and growth for both of us. Amen.

A Master Teacher?

I have been teaching a long time now.
I believe that I am effective.
I have been privileged to serve
as a supervisor for student teachers,
and a mentor for new teachers.
I have been called a master teacher.
It feels good to be confident
and to be so affirmed by others.

I want to be a master teacher.
But what does that mean?
I want it to mean that I am effective,
that I teach and my students learn, and
even that they learn to love learning.
I do not want it to mean that I am arrogant,
that I teach but no longer learn, or worse,
that I think I have nothing more to learn.

God who sent Jesus the Christ,
Jesus who is the Master Teacher,
fill me with his Spirit.
Make me effective. Make me confident.
Keep me humble. Keep me learning.

I want to be a master teacher.
God, show me what that means.
In the name of the Master Teacher. Amen.

Knowing When to Retire

God, my help in years past,
my hope for years to come,
hear my prayer for guidance
as I struggle to decide when to retire.

I have taught a long time.
I feel good about
what I have been able to give to my students.
I am thankful for
what my students have given to me.
There have been frustrations and disappointments,
but most of the time
teaching has been a meaningful vocation,
a way to give myself in service to others.
Yet I know that the time is approaching
when I need to move into the next stage of my life.
When will it be that time?
I don't want to stay too long,
past the time when I can give my best.
When will it be that time?
How will I know?

There are so many questions to be answered,
so many concerns to be considered.
What will I do? Will I have enough money?
How long will I be healthy
and able to do the things I want to do?
As my family also changes,
what will my loved ones need from me?

Holy Spirit, guide my decision-making.
Direct the dialogue going on in my mind
with the wisdom of your loving purpose for me.
Calm the anxiety simmering in my heart
with the assurance that you are near
and will care for me . . . in all the stages of my life.

Years ago, I heard your call to teach.
Give me grace to hear when you are calling me to retire
and serve you in new ways. Amen.

Saying Goodbye

Like the classroom that is full of "stuff"
accumulated over a lifetime of teaching,
my heart is full of joy and sorrow,
memories that span countless years.
I know it is time. I'm ready to move on.
But still it is hard to say goodbye.

Goodbye to the routines
that marked my days,
goodbye to the special moments
that made my days.
Goodbye to the students
whom I was privileged to teach,

goodbye to the students
from whom I learned so much.
Goodbye to colleagues
with whom I have worked,
goodbye to colleagues
who have become my friends.
Goodbye to familiar places.
Goodbye to cherished people.

God who fashioned the heavens
and guides the earth through its seasons,
God who created me and
guides me through the seasons of my life,
watch over me
during this changing of the seasons.
Give me a heart open to experience
in all of its fullness
the joy of celebrating,
and the sorrow of ending
a lifetime of teaching.
Give me words to express
what I want to say to others,
offerings of love and gratitude
for what they mean to me.

It is time. I'm ready. But still it is hard.
God, guide my goodbyes.
Amen.

Other books from The Pilgrim Press

HEALING WORDS FOR HEALING PEOPLE
Prayers and Meditations for Parish Nurses and Other Health Professionals
DEBORAH L. PATTERSON
ISBN 0-8298-1673-9/paper/112 pages/$14.00

This book is divided into original meditations and prayers, each designed to give strength and inspiration to the busy health professional in the various situations he or she encounters in daily routines.

BECOMING JESUS' PRAYER
Transforming Your Life through the Lord's Prayer
GREGORY PALMER, CINDY MCCALMONT, AND BRIAN MILFORD
ISBN 0-8298-1707-7/paper/96 pages/$10.00

Becoming Jesus' Prayer invites readers to take a new look at the Lord's Prayer—words so familiar to Christians, yet often muttered without thinking. Each chapter features a story, theological reflection, discussion questions, guidelines for weekly prayer at home and corporate prayer, and hymn suggestions.

THE PILGRIM PRESS
700 PROSPECT AVENUE EAST
CLEVELAND, OHIO 44115-1100

Phone orders: 1-800-537-3394 ◆ Fax orders: 216-736-2206

Please include shipping charges of $5.00 for the first book and $0.75 for each additional book.

Or order from our web sites at www.pilgrimpress.com and www.ucpress.com.

Prices subject to change without notice.